Mindful Tech

Mindful Tech

How to
Bring Balance to
Our Digital Lives

David M. Levy

Yale
UNIVERSITY PRESS

New Haven and London

Yale University Press books may be purchased in quantity for educational, business, or
promotional use. For information, please e-mail sales.press@yale.edu (U.S. office) or
sales@yaleup.co.uk (U.K. office).

Set in Bulmer type by Newgen North America, Austin, Texas.
Printed in the United States of America.

Library of Congress Control Number: 2015940846
ISBN 978-0-300-20831-3 (cloth : alk. paper)

A catalogue record for this book is available from the British Library.

This paper meets the requirements of ANSI/NISO Z39.48-1992 (Permanence of Paper).

10 9 8 7 6 5 4 3 2 1

For my teachers

And my students

From my students I have learned most of all

—*Pirkei Avot*

Contents

Preface
Living Fast and Slow

For decades, I have been exploring how to live a rich and meaningful life while participating in both the Fast World and the Slow World—in the fast-paced, crazy-busy, information-intensive world that has become the norm for many of us, and in the slower-paced, calmer world that we sometimes touch in moments of quiet contemplation.

I am a computer scientist by training, and for half a century I have been deeply engaged in the digital world and the tech industry. I first learned to program a computer as a teenager, in the mid-1960s, and did a significant amount of computer work in college. I went on to complete a Ph.D. in computer science and artificial intelligence at Stanford University and worked for years as a researcher at the famed Xerox Palo Alto Research Center (PARC), the Silicon Valley think tank where the networked personal computer was invented. In 2000, I moved from Silicon Valley to Seattle, from one tech mecca to another, to assume my current faculty position at the University of Washington's Information School, where I conduct research and teach about today's digital developments.

As this brief description makes clear, I know the fast-paced life of the high-tech world quite well. In many ways I have thrived in this milieu. It has allowed me to explore fascinating intellectual and technical questions while affording me a decent living. But at the same time, it has continually exposed me to the challenges of living a life in the fast lane—the stress, the sense of overload, the sinking feeling that there is no end to the acceleration, and the continual search for better coping strategies.

In parallel with this fast-paced, high-tech life, and as something of an antidote, I began to explore modes of living that were slower, calmer, and more contemplative. While in graduate school in my early twenties, I began to feel the need to get quieter. Several times, a friend took me to Bay Area zendos (Zen meditation centers), where I sat cross-legged and tried to pay attention to my breathing. I hated it. But just a few years later, while still in graduate school, I began to study Western calligraphy, the ancient art of writing with a broad-edged pen, and this practice addressed my need to do something quieter, more body-oriented, less narrowly intellectual. Post-Ph.D. I spent two years studying calligraphy full time in London.

Calligraphy was an important bridge practice for me. Whereas my earlier exposure to Zen meditation had failed to engage me, my experience with calligraphy was altogether different. Although it wasn't explicitly described this way, the effort involved in skillfully bringing pen, ink, and paper together required a great deal of attention: to the moment-to-moment interaction between body, materials, and the emerging forms. In London I found that I could spend long hours sitting at my drawing board in my little garret room, pen or quill in hand, and time seemed to disappear as I became lost in the activity. If the phone rang (which it rarely did in those days) at the end of a weekend of such work, I sometimes found that I had trouble speaking—clearly, another part of my mind was engaged. After the stresses of graduate school, I needed these Slow World practices to recover some semblance of balance—or perhaps to begin to find it, for the first time in my life. On my return to Silicon Valley after the two years in London, I was ready for a meditation practice, and searched for people who could help me. The Bay Area was a great place to get help, and I found a practice that has sustained me, and continued to guide me, all these years.

Back then, I didn't have language to describe these activities and experiences. But reflecting upon them now, more than thirty years later, I can see that calligraphy was my first contemplative practice, which trained me to focus more deeply and to bring my normally wandering mind and my body into better alignment. In the West, we tend to think that Asian calligraphy has this kind of meditative character, but it is clearly available in Western calligraphy as well. And I would suggest that any activity conducted with concentration—even email or Facebook—can bring us into greater balance, inviting greater calmness and clarity.

Fast and slow, high-tech and contemplative: from these two threads I have woven a life. It was perhaps inevitable that I would begin to ask how these two modes of being relate to each other. Are they distinct worlds, necessarily kept completely separate? Are they antagonistic to each other, and therefore incompatible? Can they be brought into dialogue with each other? The questions were personal (how can *I* embrace these two dimensions in my own life?) but also social and societal (what are *we* to make of these two powerful impulses?).

I have borrowed the terms Fast World and Slow World from the *New York Times* columnist Thomas Friedman. In his 1999 book on globalization, *The Lexus and the Olive Tree,* Friedman suggested that today "there is no more First World, Second World or Third World.

There's now just the Fast World—the world of the wide-open plain—
and the Slow World—the world of those who either fall by the wayside
or choose to live away from the plain in some artificially walled-off valley of their own, because they find the Fast World to be too fast, too
scary, too homogenizing or too demanding."[1]

I am not comfortable with the way Friedman writes about these two
worlds. In this quotation he dismisses, and apparently disdains, those
who want to live a slower life. Yet many of us long for a slower rhythm,
at least at times—not just because it is slow, but because it seems to offer certain qualities of being that are hard to come by in our rushed
and overloaded lives. Must we discount these attitudes, or those who
try to live them, because they seem antithetical to progress, at least as
understood by our current economic system? Whose idea of progress is
this, anyway? Neither am I comfortable with the way Friedman divides
the world into two neat categories, with his assumption that one must
choose one over the other. Mightn't it be possible for us to find ways to
better *integrate* fast and slow times and practices into our lives?

I first began to address these questions in writing twenty years
ago. In an article called "I'm Not Here Right Now to Take Your Call:
Technology and the Politics of Absence," which I wrote for a small
workshop of computer scientists and social scientists, I contrasted the
Slow World, contemplative practices I was cultivating with my Fast
World, high-tech life. It almost seemed, I noted, that the fast pace and
density of my work life was *engineered* to interfere with the Slow World
dimensions of my life. And I wondered whether the new information
technologies, which were being sold as tools for connection, might also
be having the opposite effect: disconnecting us from one another and
from ourselves.

From this first investigation in 1995, I continued to formulate questions: Was it true that digital technologies served as tools both of presence and connection and of absence and disconnection? How serious was the problematic side of their use and would it get worse? Why was it happening and what could be done about it? And could a more contemplative approach to human life—one concerned with the cultivation of quieter, more attentive, and more fully embodied ways of living—shed light on these technological changes, and perhaps help to steer them in healthier and more effective ways?

So when I moved to Seattle in 2000 to take a faculty position at the University of Washington Information School, these were the kinds of questions I wanted to explore. In those first years, I brought together experts in a variety of disciplines to discuss them. I organized workshops and conferences with titles like "Information, Silence, and Sanctuary," "Mindful Work and Technology," and "No Time to Think." I investigated the historical and philosophical conditions that seemed to be speeding up our culture and interfering with our "contemplative balance." And in the middle of the decade, in 2006, I was given the opportunity to create a unique course that allowed me to explore these questions and concerns in the classroom.

The book before you is the product of all these efforts. Most immediately, it derives from the course I created in 2006, with support from a fellowship that was jointly granted by the Center for Contemplative Mind in Society and the American Council of Learned Societies. The aim of the course, "Information and Contemplation," was to explore challenges such as information overload and the fragmentation of attention from a contemplative angle. Could we better understand the causes of such problems, as well as possible solutions to them, if we explored them through a contemplative lens? In the course I introduced students to various contemplative practices, including mindful breathing and walking, and we practiced together in the classroom. I also developed a series of exercises that asked students to become more aware of their use of digital technologies, to document what they were observing, to reflect on what they had documented, and to discuss their reflections with their fellow students and me.[2]

The student response to the first offering of the course was quite positive. I next approached the dean of the University of Washington Libraries and proposed teaching an informal, noncredit version of the course for librarians. She kindly consented, and within the first twelve months of developing the course I had taught it three times, once for UW students and twice for UW staff. As a next step, I began experimenting with shorter trainings for adult professionals at various universities around the country. Today I continue to teach the course in a variety of formats (most recently experimenting with online training), all the while tuning and refining it, and expanding the kind and number of exercises.

A great deal has changed since I first began exploring how to integrate Fast World and Slow World practices. For one thing, the Fast World has gotten even faster. My concerns in 1995—about the amount of email I was then receiving, about answering machines and call-waiting—seem insignificant, even laughable, in the face of today's information explosion and "always-on" lifestyle. And for a long time, it felt as if it wasn't acceptable to raise concerns about where we were headed. Fortunately, I sense that this is changing, as more of us come to realize that finding a healthy balance—understanding how to use our devices and apps to best effect, as well as when to abstain—requires us to ask probing, and sometimes critical, questions.

At the same time that it has become more acceptable to explore both the upside and the downside of our technology-fueled lives, the mindfulness movement has taken off. More and more people are discovering the benefits of adopting a more contemplative or mindful relationship to life and work. (I will use the words "contemplative" and "mindful" interchangeably in these pages, although their meanings differ in subtle ways. I particularly appreciate the way that "contemplative" suggests being thoughtful and reflective.) Ten years ago, I could worry that introducing a simple breath meditation in the workshops and conferences I was organizing would be too radical a step for the participants. Today, such practices are becoming more and more common, as various forms of mindfulness meditation are being introduced into companies, as well as into education at all levels, from kindergarten to college and graduate school (see Appendixes C and D).

As a result of these developments, questions concerning the relationship between our Fast World and Slow World lives have now entered the public discourse. And as a result of my own extended inquiry, I am now certain that we *can* mix fast and slow modes of living and working. What's more, I believe that we need to if we are going to use the new technologies in healthy and effective ways. Education and training are the keys. We need to create the space and time to observe and reflect on the ways we are using our digital tools and the effects they are having on us. And the understandings that arise from such observations and reflections can lead us to make meaningful changes. In the pages ahead, I will show you how.

Acknowledgments

This book is the product of many years of conversation and collaboration with many people who have served as my teachers, guides, colleagues, and fellow investigators. I am deeply grateful to all of them, and to the institutions that have made this inquiry possible.

The Center for Contemplative Mind in Society has played a huge role, granting me the fellowship to teach the course on which this book is based and stimulating a broad investigation into the place of contemplative practices in higher education from which I have greatly benefited. It has also created a global community of scholars and teachers from whom I have learned so much. I am particularly grateful to Mirabai Bush, Arthur Zajonc, Daniel Barbezat, Sharon Parks, and Carrie Bergman.

The Puget Sound group on Sustainability and Contemplative Practice, founded and led by Jean MacGregor, has been a tremendous source of intellectual and personal support. The gatherings of this group of local academics at the Whidbey Institute, and the friendships formed through them, have inspired and challenged me, demonstrating to me what it means to be involved in "the great work."

I have been extremely fortunate in the support I've received from my home institution, the Information School at the University of

Washington—from the faculty, staff, and students. Special thanks to Deans Mike Eisenberg and Harry Bruce, who trusted me and respected this work before it was recognized within the academy. And a warm embrace to the students who have enthusiastically joined with me in exploring a more contemplative relationship with the digital realm.

I am deeply indebted to my collaborators on the study of meditation and multitasking: to Jacob Wobbrock, Alfred Kasadiak, Marilyn Ostergren, Cynthia Kear, Michelle Fokos, and Darlene Cohen (1942–2011). Without Darlene's enthusiastic participation, in what turned out to be the last years of her life, this study would never have come about. Thanks too to the National Science Foundation (and to Ephraim Glinert) for funding the study (grant IIS-0942646), and to the John D. and Catherine T. MacArthur Foundation (and to Elspeth Revere and Kathy Im, in particular) for helping to support the initial workshops and conferences from which this work emerged.

I am grateful to those friends and teachers who have continued to teach and inspire me, and whose influence is reflected in this book: Ewan Clayton, Norman Fischer, Mike Gillespie, Julie Jacobs, Alfred Kasadiak, David Loy, Cheryl Metoyer, Ruth Ozeki, and Kimberly Richardson Sensei. A special thanks to Deborah Tannen for her friendship and wise counsel.

I extend deep appreciation as well to those who read and commented on the manuscript: to Daniel Barbezat, Hilarie Cash, Ewan Clayton, Katie Davis, Mike Gillespie, Alfred Kasadiak, Ted McCarthy, and Zari Weiss; and to the three anonymous reviewers for their insightful feedback.

I gratefully acknowledge the help of my agent, Lindsay Edgecombe, and my editor at Yale University Press, Jennifer Banks.

Finally, for their ongoing support and guidance, I say thank you to my friend Ewan Clayton and to my life partner, Zari Weiss. Thank you to Ewan for more than thirty years of conversation and collaboration, and for his extensive feedback on this book. Thank you to Zari for our shared life, *b'ahavah rabbah.*

Mindful Tech

Falling in the Fountain

The woman in the dark coat and pants strides purposefully through the indoor mall, a shopping bag in her right hand and a cell phone in her left. Oblivious to the fountain immediately in front of her, she trips on its rim and flips over, landing in the water headfirst, having executed a graceful somersault. She rises immediately, without missing a beat, and with the same purposeful demeanor climbs out of the fountain and walks away. The whole drama has taken fifteen seconds.

Even if you haven't seen this particular event, which was captured on the mall's in-house video and posted to the Web, you have no doubt witnessed other incidents of its kind. It is commonplace to see people bumping into objects or people as they walk down the street, their eyes glued to their cell phone screens. You may even have done it yourself. To be sure, it can be funny to observe such events, a moment of slapstick humor (provided, of course, that no one was hurt). But it can also be sad, as well as embarrassing (especially when it happens to us), to witness or participate in this kind of distracted behavior.[1]

Indeed, when I first happened upon the video of the woman falling into the fountain, I reacted in all these ways, finding it funny, sad, and embarrassing. But my main reaction was simply to feel the truth of the incident. For the video managed to capture and illustrate the struggle we are all now engaged in, as individuals and as a society, as we figure out how to incorporate digital devices into our lives in healthy and effective ways. The incident "speaks to our condition," as the Quakers would say.

Yes, we've come to realize that our digital devices can at times be overly engrossing, distracting, and perhaps even addictive. (Not so long ago, Blackberrys were called Crackberrys.) But if this is all they were, we'd assign them to the same category as illegal drugs and spend billions of dollars to hunt them down and destroy them. Whatever their problematic side, they are undeniably powerful and useful—and in today's world increasingly necessary. Surely, it is a remarkable thing to carry a device in our pockets that allows us to communicate instantaneously with loved ones, to read the news as it is unfolding in real time, to listen to music, and to play games. Not long ago, such possibilities lay only in the realm of science fiction, or magic. What makes these tools so powerful is how they allow us to *connect:* to extend ourselves across space and time, to project ourselves beyond our immediate circumstances. They are the latest developments in a five thousand–year-long trend, beginning with the invention of writing, which has made it possible for us to create forms of external memory and to speak to one another at a distance.

Yet it is exactly these rich and powerful capacities that are so problematic, even dangerous, today. For the more often we are somewhere else (texting with a distant friend, say), the more likely it is that we will end up in the fountain, literally or figuratively. And the greater the range of opportunities to extend ourselves, the more challenging it becomes to choose what to pay attention to at this very moment.

Using Our Attention Wisely

The challenge we now face boils down to this: Our devices have vastly extended our attentional choices, but the human attentional capacity remains unchanged. (Some would even argue that it has actually shrunk.) And so we must figure out how to make wise choices, and to figure out what constitutes a wise choice, so we can use our digital tools to their best advantage, and to ours.

But how can we go about doing this? My answer in this book is a simple one: You yourself are the source of these answers—many of them, at any rate. By paying attention to how you use your cell phone, how you handle email, how you feel when you are on Facebook or Pinterest, or when you multitask, you will be able to see which aspects of your current online practices are working well and which aren't. And seeing these clearly will allow you to make constructive changes.

A central premise of this book is that we function more effectively and more healthfully online when we are more attentive, relaxed, and emotionally balanced. This can also be stated in the negative: We operate less effectively and less healthfully when we are distracted, physically uncomfortable, and emotionally upset. And many of us now are often distracted and stressed out when we're online. The good news, though, is that we can actually do something about it. For we are all capable of becoming aware of these states of mind and body, and becoming more self-aware can lead us to greater attentiveness, physical well-being, and emotional balance.

Attention is the key. Through the exercises in this book, you will be learning to engage and strengthen two forms of attention, which I will call task focus and self-observation. Task focus is the ability to remain focused on whatever you are doing at the moment. It is the ability to maintain that focus in the face of the seemingly endless opportunities to wander somewhere else. Self-observation (or self-awareness—I will use these two terms interchangeably) is the ability to notice how you are feeling—what is going on in your mind and body—when you are doing whatever you're doing. As this kind of attention grows, you will be able to notice when your task attention has wandered, or when you are stressed out in ways that are compromising your desired outcomes or your well-being. Seeing this will allow you to take corrective action. And over longer periods of observation, you will be able to notice repeating patterns of unhelpful behavior that you can change.

While it should be obvious why having stronger task focus matters, it may seem odd to work on increasing your self-awareness. We have a strong tendency to focus outward when we're online—to focus on the email message we're composing and the task it addresses, on our latest Facebook posts and the people they connect us to, on our Google search for hotels in the Denver area. In this outer-directed focus, we are often impatient and rushing ahead. If a page fails to load in our Web browser quickly enough, we will quickly switch to another application. Operating in this way, there is no room to notice what is happening in our mind and body—no room to see, for example, that our left foot has fallen asleep, that our shoulders are tight and our breathing shallow, or that we're feeling anxious and distracted. Yet noticing such things, as we will see, can provide a great deal of useful information—information that may increase our understanding of our current online tendencies and habits, and can serve as the basis for making valuable changes.

But I don't expect you to take my word on this. Nor would I want you to. The only way to find out if this method of self-observation and reflection actually works is to try it for yourself.

Improving Our Digital Craft

Becoming more attentive, relaxed, and emotionally stable: It should hardly be surprising if this is a prescription for living a better online life. After all, these qualities generally contribute to greater effectiveness, and to a better quality of life, no matter what we're doing. In fact, in some areas of human life, people are explicitly trained to operate this way. Take sports, for example: To play well, the batter or the tennis player needs to be focused, not distracted. She needs a relaxed, not a tense, body to respond fluidly to the position of the ball. And she needs to be in a stable, positive state of mind, minimizing emotional disturbance. Similarly, in the handcrafts and the martial arts, the practitioner learns to approach the task at hand with a well-tuned mind and body.

Why shouldn't we approach our online activities with the same orientation to training and wholehearted engagement? Douglas Engelbart, one of the central figures in the development of personal computing, thought so. The inventor of the mouse as well as the first operational hypertext system, Engelbart used to argue that working on a computer should be likened to playing a musical instrument. And he expressed dissatisfaction with some of the ways that his ideas were taken up (and, he felt, misunderstood) in Silicon Valley.

Some of his engineers moved from SRI, where Engelbart's lab was located, to the Xerox Palo Alto Research Center in the early 1970s. And there they contributed to the creation of the Alto, the first networked personal computer, and its "user-friendly" graphical user interface. For years afterward, Engelbart argued against user-friendliness as a central design goal. Musical instruments, he claimed, weren't user-friendly. They weren't designed, first and foremost, for ease of use. Rather, they were designed for peak performance. They were designed to be played by skilled craftspeople who were intent upon improving their skills. From his point of view, a low entry cost to use was much less important than creating a powerful instrument that one could master over time.

Most of us have acquired our digital skills through a gradual process of experimentation and adaptation. And in many ways this has served us well. But we may not have imagined that it is possible to further improve these skills through a process that parallels the kind of learning we have done in sports or craftwork. Skills are learned or acquired behaviors, which can be improved through practice, observation, and reflection. I experienced this for myself in the two years I studied Western calligraphy intensively in London. I spent many hours practicing the craft—writing with a broad-edged pen or a quill, practicing the letter shapes and developing a rhythmical flow—in preparation for those times when I would produce a finished piece of work. And throughout my studies, my teachers critiqued my work, helping me not only to see more clearly what I had produced (the letters, the space between them, the overall design of the piece), but calling my attention to how I held the pen, how I breathed, how I sat and moved my body.

You may never have done calligraphy (and may never want to), but my guess is that you have engaged in just this kind of learning to improve your performance in a sport or a craft, or in playing a musical instrument. You have improved your skill not only by practicing, but by observing and reflecting upon your performance, either alone or with others. When it comes to email (or texting, or using Facebook, or any of the other myriad activities we engage in online), we are in a sense practicing all the time: we are spending *lots* of time doing it. But despite the well-known maxim, practice doesn't necessarily make perfect, at least not by itself. If our email game isn't improving, it may be because we haven't been actively *learning* how to do better, through observation and reflection. It is one of the central aims of the exercises in this book to bring these missing elements into the picture.

You may not have thought of using email or playing tennis as a craft. So allow me to explain how and why I've chosen to use this word. In English, we sometimes talk about "crafting" something, as when I say that I'm crafting a response to someone's message. Crafting here basically means "making or doing something skillfully." When I suggest we think of our online activity as craft, I certainly mean to call attention to the skill involved. But I also mean to highlight three additional dimensions of craftwork, making four in all: intention, care, skill, and learning.

Intention: When we craft something, we set out purposefully to make or do something. We have a direction and perhaps even an outcome in mind—to construct a bookcase, to play a certain piece of music or a game of tennis. But all too often do we click around aimlessly online. By clarifying our intention, and by reminding ourselves of it (or consciously changing it, when appropriate) we increase our chances of arriving successfully at our destination.

Care: When we craft something, we also care about what we are creating or performing. Care, of course, goes hand in hand with intention. We care enough to clarify our intention, and then to make sure that we are realizing it to the best of our ability.

Skill: While having a caring attitude and the best of intentions is necessary, it isn't sufficient. We also need the appropriate skills to realize our intention, including the ability to maintain and use our tools well, and to bring the best of our mind and body to the task at hand. If we pay attention to our online craft, we will be able to notice when we are proceeding skillfully, and when we're not.

Learning: Finally, if we care enough for the quality of our outcome to bring our best skills to bear, then we will want to improve these skills. This requires a commitment of time and attention, to engage in an ongoing process of learning, which is what the exercises in this book are all about.

Craft played an important role in everything Steve Jobs accomplished, and he too was introduced to it through calligraphy. In his 2005 commencement address at Stanford, he talked about his discovery of the practice in college. "Reed College at that time offered perhaps the best calligraphy instruction in the country. Throughout the campus every poster, every label on every drawer, was beautifully hand calligraphed. . . . I decided to take a calligraphy class to learn how to do this. I learned about serif and sans serif typefaces, about varying the amount of space between different letter combinations, about what makes great typography great. It was beautiful, historical, artistically subtle in a way that science can't capture, and I found it fascinating." This exposure to calligraphy directly affected the design of the Macintosh computer—"If I had never dropped in on that single course in college," Jobs said, "the Mac would have never had multiple typefaces or proportionally spaced fonts." But beyond the specifics of letterforms and spacing, Jobs clearly absorbed the craft perspective. Through his leadership, Apple applied this perspective to its devices and their user interfaces, creating not just highly functional but beautiful products. Similarly, I believe that we can craft online practices and experiences that are more functional and artful, if not beautiful.[2]

Does this sound like I'm suggesting we all become as obsessively perfectionistic as Steve Jobs famously was, that we become Olympic-level email and Facebook users? This is by no means my intention. Rather, these four dimensions of craft—intention, care, skill, and learning—point us in a direction, not to a final outcome. By being more intentional in our online activities, by caring enough to spend that time well, by engaging mind, body, tools, and materials skillfully, and by spending time in learning through observation and reflection, we can avoid a certain amount of the mindless and stressful behavior that is now so common in our online lives. Ultimately, you will decide how much of this work you do, and when. Even small increments in your learning can have significant, positive consequences.

I once heard a talk by someone who'd helped found the macrobiotics movement, which promoted a lean, grain-and-local-vegetable-based diet. He complained that later adherents had taken the diet too strictly and seriously. "Sometimes," I recall him saying, "you just have to eat a Snickers bar." As one of my students exclaimed: "Aren't we allowed twenty minutes a day to let our mind and clicking hand wander and not judge the way in which our time is spent?" We certainly are, in my opinion. The challenge and the opportunity is to decide for ourselves when to engage with intention and care, and when to eat the Snickers bar (and when, sometimes, to eat the Snickers bar with intention and care). And when we decide to act intentionally and carefully, we ought to feel confident that our craft skills are up to the task.

Your Discoveries and Insights Are Central

What makes this approach unique is that it aims to give you the tools to make your own discoveries. If you want to learn how to manage your email more productively, you can find endless Web sites offering you the three rules of good email usage, or the five principles for coping with email overload. Or you can find sites that will teach you particular techniques—how to limit the number of messages in your inbox, for example. You can also find a variety of software tools that will help you manage your email. (To see for yourself, do a Web search on a phrase like "email overload.") There's no question that many of these approaches have value. But why are there so many different choices? The answer, quite simply, is that no single approach works well for everyone. One size does not fit all. You can certainly learn valuable lessons by observing what other people do (as you will see in the pages ahead), but in the end it is up to you to craft an approach that satisfies your own unique needs, and your own cognitive and emotional makeup. And you can't do that without a clear sense of *your* needs, *your* makeup, and *your* habitual patterns of behavior.

But there is another reason why making our own discoveries is a valuable strategy. Throughout our lives, most of us have been regularly told what to do, how to behave, and what to believe by parents, teachers, and other authority figures. Stand up straight, come to class on time, don't speak with your mouth full. But for the most part, being told "I know what's best for you" simply doesn't work. While such statements may point us to areas of our lives that we should investigate, they can't substitute for the discoveries that we ourselves make, and therefore come to own. When we see our habits and patterns for ourselves, we are in a better position to make meaningful changes.

Beyond Individual Change

So this book will focus on what you, as an individual, can discover and change. This is the arena where each of us has the greatest leverage. But it is not the only place where change can happen. Meaningful changes can, and sometimes must, also happen in the realm of the social and political (through collective action) and in the realm of the technological (by making changes to the technologies we use).

To see this, let's return to the use of cell phones. On the individual level, each of us can make choices about when and how we use our cell phones—whether or not we answer our phone during a meeting or text while we're walking. But on the social and political level, we come together as groups, and at times as an entire society, to establish norms, ethical principles, and laws to place limits on what we can and can't do. Thus in recent years there has been a growing consensus in the United States that some uses of cell phones are too dangerous to be left up to individual choice, and an increasing number of states have enacted legislation setting limits on what drivers can do with their phones. Drivers, of course, are still free to break the law (and many do), but the risk of a moving violation is meant to serve as a warning and a deterrent. Changes to the technologies we use, much like shared agreements and legislation, also aim to effect collective change. But unlike normative or legal forms of regulation, they sometimes contain within themselves the means of enforcement and thus limit individual choice. A recent *New York Times* story, for example, describes a technological system that would block texts and prevent phone calls from reaching a driver.[3]

Although the focus in this book is squarely on the individual—on what you yourself can do—it is my hope that the work done at this level will also provide insights that are useful for making broader social and technological changes. Ultimately, these three levels can't be fully separated. As you come to better understand your own behavior, you are likely to see how it is affected by and in turn affects the behavior of others (the social level), and how it has been shaped by the decisions that the designers of the tools have made (the technological level).

Why do I say this? Beyond enabling you to make better use of your digital tools, it is my hope that this book will help you to be a more informed consumer, and perhaps even a better citizen. So many of the discussions we are now having about the digital world tend to be based around simplistic dualisms. We ask whether texting is good or bad for us, or whether the Internet is making us smart or stupid. But when we can look at the richness of our own experience online, we have the chance to discover when and how texting is helpful and when it isn't, or when being online is productive and illuminating and when it isn't. And especially if we are doing this work with others (in a classroom or a work group setting), we can see that the choices others make for the skillful use of their tools aren't necessarily the same as our own. Seeing our similarities and differences, and noticing the complexities (and even contradictions) within ourselves, will make us better partners in

the collective conversation we ought to have about social and technological change.

How to Use This Book

The book is meant to be used both by individuals working alone and
by groups of people working together. Because the contents emerged
from classroom (and therefore group) use, I am most familiar with the
kinds of learning that are possible in group settings. While one of the
strengths of this approach is that it allows people to come to their own,
unique understanding of their online behavior and to craft their own
unique changes, I have seen again and again how the learning is greatly
amplified when people share their insights with one another. So even if
you decide to work alone, I hope you will find a way to engage others
in your process, perhaps sharing your written reflections with them, or
talking with them about the discoveries you are making.

It is also possible to read through the entire book without performing any of the exercises (performing some of the exercises later,
or not at all). Toward the end of each of the exercise chapters, I describe the kinds of discoveries that others have made and quote from
my students' reflections. So even if you don't do the exercises, you may
find that reading other people's insights suggests changes that you
might make.

All of my teaching experience is with undergraduates and with
adults (both graduate students and working adults). But I suspect that
the exercises are usable or adaptable for younger students as well—
students in high school and possibly earlier. If you are a K–12 teacher
interested in making use of the book in your class (or a parent wanting to use it with your children), I suggest you first do the exercises

yourself—all the better if you can do them collaboratively with other teachers or parents.

All of the quotations from students are real, not paraphrases. I have obtained my students' permission to quote them, and have changed their names and obscured their identities. Although most of them (roughly 80 percent) were enrolled in the course on Information and Contemplation I teach at the University of Washington Information School, their ages range from late teens to fifties, and many of them have had real jobs in the world, or were holding down real jobs while in school. Thus thinking of these people simply as students misrepresents their various stages in life. When referring to them, I have chosen not to distinguish between those officially enrolled in UW courses and those who took informal (noncredit) courses with me, either online or in person.

A Word About Language

A word too about my use of language. Throughout the book, I talk about making changes to our digital practices that are "healthy and effective." Nowhere, however, do I explicitly say what I mean by these words. In fact, I leave it up to you, as an integral part of the exploration you will be doing, to decide for yourself what constitutes healthy and effective behavior. This strategy works quite well, I've found, in my courses. Just by paying attention to what we are doing and how it makes us feel, we can discover how to operate more skillfully and in the service of greater well-being.

Throughout the book I also use phrases like "being online" and "our online lives." But what exactly does it mean to be online these days—and what does it mean to be offline? The extremes seem clear enough: When you are on your laptop (as I am now), and working on multiple applications with an Internet connection, we can probably all agree that you are online. And when you are sitting at the beach reading a physical book with no cell phone or Internet coverage, you are definitely offline. But suppose that you are working on a laptop without an Internet connection, or you are listening to music stored on your smart phone? Does "online" simply mean using a digital device, technology, or application, or does it perhaps mean using it in a certain mode?

There are no definitive answers to such questions, because "online" and "offline" are terms of art in our current cultural conversation, and they lack absolute or clear boundaries. I choose to use them here in exactly this way—as rough and inexact pointers to certain activities and behaviors we are all now engaged in. In the end what matters isn't how I or you use these words, but what you discover when you look carefully at the specific behaviors and practices that constitute your online and offline life.

My guess is that notions of being online and offline will become less significant as the digital revolution matures and digital connectivity is increasingly woven into more and more aspects of our daily lives. What will become more important is how well or poorly we are engaged with whatever we're doing. And it is just this—the quality of our engagement—that we will be exploring in this book.

And a Word About Attitude

Finally, I want to say a few words about the attitude with which I hope you will approach the exercises. I think of them as experiments—certainly not scientific experiments in the classical sense but rather personal investigations in which you get to play a double role: as the performer (the experimental subject) and the observer. You are first and foremost the performer, in each exercise engaging in your primary practice: using email or checking Facebook, switching among multiple tasks and applications, or abstaining from one or more digital practices. But you are also the observer, the investigator, whose job it is to closely study what the performer is doing.

To play the role of observer well, it will help to be curious, honest, and nonjudgmental. To be curious is to be genuinely interested in what you're seeing. To be honest is to care enough to see things as they are. And to be nonjudgmental is to be willing to suspend judgment—especially, in this case, *self*-judgment—which can make it hard to accept what you are seeing. For in paying close attention to your online behavior, you are likely to observe yourself doing unskillful and unhelpful things. And this may well provoke self-criticism, which can reduce your ability to investigate clearly and honestly. The challenge in allowing your curiosity full rein is to look honestly at things you don't like without being too hard on yourself. Keep in mind: if you weren't sometimes engaging online in counterproductive ways, there would be little to improve.

Observing Our Online Lives

It is 9:15 AM on Monday and I've just arrived at my favorite coffee-house. My plan is to spend the next couple of hours working on this book. I feel rested and alert, and ready to get down to work. With my cappuccino on the tabletop to my left, I open the chapter I was last editing. I also open my email inbox—*just to check,* I tell my-self. Glancing at my inbox, I see my various obligations—those left over from the previous week, as well as those new messages that have arrived since I checked email on my smart phone before I left home. My eye goes immediately to the header of a troubling message. It's the second reminder (or is it the third?) of a task I'd agreed to complete a week ago and have been putting off.

Barely aware of the anxiety this has provoked in me and without any conscious intent, I've suddenly opened a Web browser and begun to scan the *New York Times* online. *Gee, I wonder whether there's any interesting news,* I'm thinking to myself. *Oh yes, a new data breach at a major American corporation, more violence in the Middle East ...* After a couple of minutes of scrolling and skimming, I catch myself in this act of procrastination, chiding myself for allowing myself to be diverted. *I really ought to respond to my colleague's message,* I tell myself guiltily. And so I open her message and begin to read through it, seriously this time (as opposed to last week, when I'd merely skimmed it).

But before I've gotten through the first paragraph, on the periphery of my awareness I hear a beep and see the visual signal alerting me to the arrival of a new email message. I glance at the header long enough to identify the recipient and the subject matter and decide that I can let it slide for now. I return to my colleague's message.

I've just started rereading the first paragraph when my cell phone rings. Fumbling in my backpack to find it, I glance at the screen to see that it's from my wife, whom I just saw twenty minutes ago. My first thought is to wonder whether everything is all right. *I'd better find out,* I think, and answer the call. She's contacting me, I learn, to ask me to add one more item to the grocery list for the shopping I'll be doing on my way home that evening. *Geez,* I think, *couldn't she just have texted me or sent me email, rather than interrupting me like this? Doesn't she know how* busy *I am?* She knows me well enough, of course, to pick up on the hint of tension in my voice as I tell her I'll take care of it. "What's wrong?" she asks. "I'm just trying to get some work done," I say somewhat testily. "Look, I'm sorry," she says, "I'll talk to you later."

Once again I return to reading the email message I've been avoiding for a week, and this time I'm able to read it through to completion.

Clearly my morning hasn't begun all that well. I had set out with a clear intention, to work on a book chapter, and was ready to do just that. But now, after just a few minutes of seemingly minor activity, I still haven't begun, and have even lost some of my enthusiasm and my composure. Not only have I allowed myself to be distracted by other events, but I'm a bit stressed out, which is reflected in my posture (a bit slunk down) and my shallow, rapid breathing.

Reflecting on What Happened

So what just happened? Nothing much, really: a cascade of small reactions, building one upon the other. Asked to summarize these first few moments of my workday, I might say something like, "Well, I read an email message I'd been avoiding and took a call from my wife about the grocery shopping." But what's missing from this description is the complex work I was continually doing from moment to moment to decide what to pay attention to next and for how long, and how to handle the different emotions that were arising in the process. Making a different set of minor choices might have set my day off on a very different course.

Let's begin by noticing how I was regularly shifting my task focus: from my colleague's email message to the *New York Times* Web site, then back to my colleague's message, then to the newly arriving email message, to my cell phone, and so on. Each of these shifts represented a decision on my part, about which task to pay attention to next and thus what to do next. Some of these decisions were under my conscious control—they represented strategic decisions based on my intention at the moment. Thus, I chose to shift back from the *New York Times* to my colleague's message because my intention was to stop avoiding it—to stop procrastinating. Once I'd seen that the incoming phone call was from my wife, I consciously chose to answer it. And once the call had ended, I consciously chose to return to my colleague's message and to read it all the way through.

Some of my decisions, however, were unconscious, or were at best semiconscious. They were more like habitual, knee-jerk reactions than willed decisions. I switched over to the *New York Times* Web site and began scanning it before I realized what I was doing. I switched there in spite of my intention to engage with my colleague's message. When my cell phone rang, I reached for it largely out of unconscious habit, a Pavlovian response to the sound of the ring. And as a result of this cascade of decisions and reactions, I completely lost sight of my original intention, to do some writing and editing.

Let's also notice how my emotional reactions played a part in how I deployed my attention, and thus how the action unfolded. What led me to open my email first thing, despite my intention to begin working on the book? I felt anxious about what might be waiting for me there—hence the impulse "just to check." This combined with the difficulty I often experience when I first sit down to write, a kind of performance anxiety, and led me to divert my attention elsewhere. Anxiety was also at work, along with a dose of guilt, when I switched to the *New York Times* Web site upon seeing my colleague's reminder message. At some level I felt "get me out of here," and I took off in search of something more interesting—another act of avoidance and escape. (Other people might use Facebook or Twitter in this way, but my go-to distractions are generally email and the news.) I also experienced some distress when I felt that my wife's phone call was unnecessarily disruptive. But my annoyance at her call was compounded by the challenging emotions I was already feeling. Thus, driven by largely unconscious emotional reactions, I bounced around among various apps, Web sites, and devices. None of these behaviors caused any real damage, but they weren't particularly skillful or productive either.

My body, too, was a participant in this little online drama. (How could it not have been, since it was the vehicle through which my actions were being performed?) It was registering and reflecting the quality of my experience, as bodies inevitably do, including the effects of my largely unrecognized emotional reactions. My collapsed posture and shallow breathing at the end were indicators of the stress I was now feeling. And had I been more observant of my body's reactions while these events were unfolding—the catch in my breath when I first saw my colleague's message or the tightening of my throat and shoulders when I talked with my wife—I might have had a better chance of recognizing how I was reacting and steered a different course.

Anxiety, guilt, annoyance, collapsed posture, and shallow breathing: All these states of mind and body were reflections of what was going on for me in these few minutes of online activity. And they were also determinants of that activity, leading me to respond in ways that weren't always helpful. Had I been able to exercise greater self-awareness—noticing, for example, the anxiety over my colleague's message and deciding not to switch over to the *New York Times*—I might have avoided more of the unnecessary and unhelpful detours I took. I might have steered a more conscious and effective course through the field of choices that arose.

To be sure, there is nothing exceptional in this small sequence of actions and reactions—certainly it has none of the dramatic power of the woman falling into the fountain. But that is exactly the point. We are all continually making moment-to-moment microdecisions like these, both online and offline, about what to pay attention to, what to ignore, and how to manage the thoughts and feelings, the bodily movements, postures, and breathing that inevitably accompany these decisions. And it is from the accumulation of such microdecisions that the fabric of our days is woven. The productivity and character of my day will now partly depend on what has just happened—on what I have and haven't done, and how I now feel about it. And it will also depend on the decisions I make from this moment on (whether to return to writing or to my colleague's long overdue request), as well as on the quality of engagement (the state of my mind and my body) that I bring to whatever I choose to do.

And what about you? How do you decide what to pay attention to, and when? Are you aware of the decisions you are making and your basis for making them? How do your emotional reactions shape your choices? How does the state of your body reflect and influence these choices? And overall, when are the choices you are making, consciously or unconsciously, in the service of your intentions and your best interests, and when aren't they? These are the kinds of questions I will be encouraging you to explore in the pages ahead as you inquire into the quality and character of your online life.

You won't need to engage in the minutely detailed, moment-to-moment observation that I've just illustrated—unless you're drawn to this level of careful analysis, as I am. But you will need to tune your eye and your mind to observe more closely what you are doing, and how you feel while doing it. This may initially seem strange or even uncomfortable. We're not used to observing in this way, least of all when we're online. It hasn't occurred to us that we might examine our habits of body and mind, or that there might be much value in doing so. Mostly we are charging (and sometimes limping) forward, just trying to keep up with the volume of our work and the pace of our lives.

But once we observe and reflect, we can begin to see the kinds of choices we habitually make and why we make them. We are then in a position to evaluate these patterns. And it is a small step further to imagine alternative ways of behaving and to develop personal guidelines.

Overview of the Exercises

The route to this learning is through a sequence of five exercises. Exercises 1 and 2 (in Chapters 4 and 5) ask you to engage with a single application, email—or, if you prefer, Facebook or texting. Exercise 1 (observing email) directs you simply to observe your current practice, paying attention to what is happening in your mind and body at different points in order to become more familiar with your current habits and what lies behind them. Exercise 2 (focused email) asks you to try something new: to use email (or Facebook or texting) in a more focused way than perhaps you normally do and to observe what happens. It asks you to experiment with a method that engages and strengthens your task focus.

In Exercises 3 and 4 (in Chapters 6 and 7), you move from exploring a single application to multitasking: switching among multiple tasks, devices, and applications. Exercise 3 (observing multitasking) is once again purely observational: you will simply pay attention to your current multitasking habits and patterns and to your experience while you are thus engaged. Exercise 4 (focused multitasking) then asks you to experiment with multitasking in a more task-focused way and to notice the effects, both on the quality of your results and on your sense of well-being.

Exercise 5 (in Chapter 8) directs you to abstain from one or more of your digital practices—to unplug from certain applications or devices of your own choosing and to notice the effects of this unplugging on your mind and body.

Each of the exercises follows the same six-part structure:

Step 1: You *perform* the primary practice (attending to your email, Facebook, or texting; engaging in multitasking; or unplugging from one or more apps or devices).

Step 2: You *observe* what you are doing and feeling, paying special attention to what is happening in your mind and body as you engage in your primary practice.

Step 3: You *log* what you are observing, maintaining a written record of what you have been noticing.

Step 4: You *consolidate* your observations, reviewing your log and summarizing what you've been noticing.

Step 5: You *formulate* personal guidelines, making use of your consolidated observations to propose changes to your primary practice.

Step 6: You *share* and discuss your discoveries with others, learning more about your practice (as well as other people's practices) in the process.

While you are free to pick and choose among the exercises, I strongly suggest that you begin with Chapter 4, Observing Email, which is designed as the entryway to the whole sequence. (Or, if you decide not to start here, I recommend that you read through Chapter 4 before tackling any of the others.) This is always the first exercise I offer in my course and it has two main purposes. One, of course, is to help you learn more about whatever digital practice you've decided to explore. The other is to help familiarize you with the method of self-observation that you will be using in all the exercises. In addition, it is in this chapter that I give the most detailed explanation of the six-step structure that is common to all the exercises.

Taking Charge of Our Online Lives

In performing these exercises, people regularly discover that they can take greater charge of their online lives. They come to see how they've allowed their online activities to be governed by unexamined rules and expectations, as well as unconscious habits. And they realize that they actually have much greater choice in the matter. Some things they can change. But even when they can't change certain external conditions (such as the amount of email they receive), they still have the possibility of changing their reaction to or their relationship with these conditions. This is the power that bringing greater attention, or mindfulness, to our lives offers us. Diane, one of my students, who had come back to school after working in the tech industry, sums it up this way:

> What mindfulness really is to me is the ability to direct your
> attention where you want it to go—to have a choice. . . . The
> idea that "mindfulness" is really a word for choosing what to pay
> attention to is incredibly empowering. In a world where we are
> surrounded by advertisements, sales pitches, the biggest, best,
> and brightest promises of happiness and fulfillment that money
> can buy, not to mention the near constant information overload of

emails, status updates, tweets, photo albums, Netflix queues, RSS feeds, playing whack-a-mole with phone notifications . . . Sometimes you just want to check out, right? I wish I could say that we could get away, but I don't think that as a society we can, or even that we should. Technology is an equalizer, and gives voice to those who previously did not have one. In its most ideal state, the Internet is truly democratic, but that means that the world just got a lot noisier because so many more voices are now being heard. Being able to direct your attention, and choose what to pay attention to, is, I believe, an essential coping mechanism to deal with all of these new voices, all these new things that are demanding our attention. When we are mindful we choose to pay attention to what is explicitly important to us; being mindful begins to reveal our values in a way wandering lost through the digital landscape can never do.

Attention, Emotions, and the Body

W
e operate more effectively online, I proposed in Chapter 1, when we are more attentive, relaxed, and emotionally balanced. And we can *learn* to be more attentive, relaxed, and emotionally balanced, I further suggested, through self-observation and awareness: by noticing what is happening in our mind and body while we're online, by noticing when and why we become distracted, stressed out, and upset, and by using this understanding to adjust and tune our digital craft. In the exercises beginning next chapter, you will have a chance to try out this kind of self-observation for yourself. But before we get there, I want to look more closely at the importance of attention, the emotions, and the body for the health and effectiveness of our online lives.

Two Modes of Attention

"Everyone knows what attention is," William James, the founder of American psychology, wrote in 1890, devoting an entire chapter to the subject in his book *The Principles of Psychology*. "It is the taking possession by the mind, in clear and vivid form, of one out of what seem several simultaneously possible objects or trains of thought." And its opposite is distraction, a "confused, dazed, scatterbrained state." While we all know from experience what attention and distraction are, research on the brain, most of which has been conducted in the hundred years since James wrote these words, has helped to explain the mechanisms that underlie both of these states. Our propensity for distraction, it turns out, arises from a central feature of the human attentional system, which is crucial for our survival. For while we need the ability to focus narrowly on one thing, we also need the ability to remain open to interruptions, and thus to potential distractions.[1]

Human attention is, among other things, a focusing mechanism. It involves systems that make it possible for us to select an object—an event, a person, a sight, a sound, or a sensation—from all the stimuli potentially available to us at any one time. We might think of focused attention as a flashlight beam that can be used to explore a dark room. Point it this way and you will see the armchair in the corner. Move it slightly to the right and you will see the side table and the lamp resting on it. The beam is highly selective: whatever isn't within its immediate path is invisible to our conscious awareness, or it shades into darkness. We employ this selection mechanism when we listen intently to music or to a friend, or when we engage in deep, concentrated reading.

But human attention operates in another mode as well. Not only can it narrow down to focus on a single object, it can open up, becoming receptive to what's going on in the surrounding environment. (Imagine a flashlight that has two settings: one that focuses an intense beam in a small region, the other that bathes a larger space in a diffuse light, allowing us to take in a great deal more, but with less visual acuity.) We employ this kind of open attention when we take in a broad swath of our environment, without resting our focus on any one object in particular. Writing these words, for example, I have been narrowly focused on what I've been trying to communicate. But I am pausing now to open my attention to what is happening both inside and around me: I hear the hum and chatter of other people in the café, I feel the pressure of my palms on the laptop keyboard, I notice the rhythm of my breathing. (Both of these modes, focused and open, are what James calls "attention." When he uses the word "distraction," he is referring to those states of mind we all know only too well: when we are "confused, dazed, scatterbrained"—when we are unable to focus with any clarity on a single thing or on our inner or outer environment.)[2]

As the flashlight analogy suggests, these two modes can be engaged exclusive of each other. It is possible to focus so narrowly on a single object that you block out all awareness of your surroundings. And it is possible to be so caught up in the swirl of sensory and perceptual events that you aren't really able to notice any one thing. Most of the time, however (this is where the flashlight analogy breaks down), we are operating in a mixed attentional mode: somewhat focused and somewhat open. The challenge we face is how to employ both of these modes skillfully when we're online.

All creatures exhibit both of these abilities, to some degree. Living organisms need to be able to focus intently on their prey while stalking it, and at the same time to remain sufficiently open to their surroundings to avoid other predators. Most of us today don't live with these kinds of threats, but we still require both of these attentional modes to get through our day. Think about crossing a busy street. You need to be able to focus on getting to the other side. But you also have to remain aware of your surroundings, on the lookout for threats, such as a car or bicycle that runs the light.

Attentional Shift, Attentional Choice

So when we're on our computer, phone, or tablet, we are typically in a mixed attentional state. The challenge is to figure out how to deploy our attention, how best to deploy our task focus (focused attention) and our self-awareness (open attention). This means keeping in mind what our current intention is, what we're trying to accomplish, so we don't just drift aimlessly. It also means skillfully handling the interruptions that will inevitably occur.

Fortunately, we have a certain amount of control: at times we can consciously choose what to focus on. If I were to ask you to pay attention to the sensations in your left foot right now, you could probably do that. You could will yourself to direct the flashlight beam of your attention to your foot. But if a car were suddenly to backfire loudly a few feet away, you would startle and orient to the sound. And this would happen without any conscious control on your part. The brain, it turns out, has two different attentional systems. The top-down system is under conscious control. It's what allows you to focus on something at will. The bottom-up system, an earlier evolutionary development, is completely automated. Its job is to scan the environment for potential threats, alerting us to them whether we want that information or not. We can't turn off this alerting mechanism—it is essentially hard-wired into us.[3]

Interruptions come in two varieties. External interruptions are the sounds, smells, movements, and physical contact that our senses pick up from the world around us: the ringing phone, the knock on the door, the hand on the shoulder, the pop-up ad that suddenly shows up on the screen. Internal interruptions arise from within our own minds and bodies. We feel hunger pangs, or suddenly remember that we're due at the dentist. We read an email message and feel anxious, we feel a sudden pain in our neck.

Much of the time the mind seems to have a mind of its own. We aren't in charge—if "we" here means the conscious, willful self. Indeed, recent neuroscience, as well as the experience of meditators, suggests that the mind's "default" mode is a kind of inner monologue. When we aren't focusing on something, we are generally talking to ourselves, telling ourselves stories about what has happened in the past, or what we imagine will take place in the future. During such times, which seem to occur quite frequently, we aren't present to what's happening immediately around us—we are "lost in thought." (Being lost in thought—caught up in our internal mind chatter—is an example of what James means by "distraction.")[4]

Although we can't simply turn off the alerting mechanism, there are ways that we can minimize distractions when we're working on-line. By observing the conditions under which we normally operate and their effect on us, we can discover which of these conditions limit our effectiveness and do something about them—closing down unnecessary applications and turning off our phones, for example. But we can't eliminate all interruptions—least of all those that are internally generated, those thoughts and feelings that seemingly arise on their own. What we can do, however, is notice them as they arise and make skillful decisions about how to proceed in the face of them—whether to respond to them in the moment (and if so, how) or to ignore them.

In other words, by strengthening our self-awareness, we can increase the possibility of exercising choice, and thus avoiding largely unconscious reactions.

Multitasking as an Attentional Practice

Attention lies at the heart of the practice we call multitasking. Although it is often assumed that multitasking means attending to several things at the same time, it is now clearly established that we can mainly focus on only one thing at a time. Thus when we are reading our email while talking on the phone, we are actually shifting our attention back and forth between the two tasks—we are moving the narrow beam of our flashlight from our email to our conversational partner and back again to our email. But at the same, we are also typically maintaining a degree of open attention, which will allow us to notice other interesting attentional opportunities as they arise. And at those moments that we are faced with more than one potential object of attention, we have the possibility of choosing which one to focus on. (These three attentional functions—focused attention, open attention, and choice—correspond rather closely to three brain networks that neuroscientists have identified: those concerned with orienting, alerting, and conflict-resolution.)[5]

Of course, we can get ourselves into trouble in a variety of ways while multitasking. (How many of us have gotten caught out reading our email while talking to our partner or to a friend?) Sometimes, multitasking is more like "multiflailing," to borrow a term coined by one of my students. Our attentional strength is weak, and we aren't actually focusing deeply or carefully on anything. And we aren't making informed choices about what to attend to next—indeed, we may not be consciously choosing at all. Under such circumstances, we are engaging in distraction rather than consciously crafting our online activity.

Multitasking can also be challenging because, in a strict engineering sense, it is inefficient. The sequential shifting of focused attention takes time. The brain needs processing time to disengage from its current object of focus and to engage with another. Using an economic metaphor, psychologists call the time spent shifting between objects "switch costs." The more often we switch between objects, then, the more time is spent in the switching activity itself and the less time paying attention to our task or activity.[6]

But the kind of open attention that allows the mind to flit from one thing to another can also be quite valuable. Assuming that attention always needs to be narrowly focused on achieving some goal "downplays the fruitfulness of the mind's tendency to drift whenever left to its own devices," Daniel Goleman says. Indeed, at times, "a mind adrift lets our creative juices flow." Sometimes clicking around between sites and devices, wandering here and there, can be a fruitful practice. It all depends on when and how we do it.

There is currently a debate about the value and place of multitasking, as you will see in Chapters 6 and 7. I believe that multitasking has its place in today's complex world, especially when performed skillfully and at appropriate times. The skills that we will be exploring in this book—for strengthening task focus, self-awareness, and the ability to make wise attentional choices—are exactly those that can help us not only multitask more successfully but decide when (and when not) to multitask.

Emotions and the Stress Response

For decades it has been clear that being online sometimes brings out the worst in people. Perhaps it's the anonymity—as a famous *New Yorker* cartoon noted in the 1990s, "On the Internet, nobody knows you're a dog." Or perhaps it is the lack of face-to-face feedback that encourages people to act out in ways they might not in person. Regardless, there are times when people erupt emotionally online, and with a frequency that has led to the coining of terms such as "flaming" and "trolling" to describe varieties of out-of-control online behavior.

These are the violent outbursts and tantrums of online life, and it isn't hard to see how disruptive they can be. But these are relatively rare. What is much more common, and perhaps more challenging to our everyday digital pursuits, is the constant play of low-level emotions— such as anxiety, frustration, and anger—that arise as we check email or Facebook, as we surf the Web and text our friends. Indeed, many of us today seem to be regularly stressed out and emotionally on edge when we're online. It isn't hard to understand why: We live rushed lives. We feel burdened by what we're doing, don't feel we have enough time to devote to our work and our personal lives, and live with a sense of frustration and anxiety about getting things done.

Of course, emotions are an unavoidable dimension of human existence. And they are tremendously valuable. Positive emotions such as love, joy, and contentment not only make life worthwhile but motivate us to reach out to others and to engage with the world in helpful and meaningful ways. And negative emotions, which arise through the bottom-up alerting system I noted earlier, are an essential component of the survival mechanism we have inherited from our reptilian and mammalian ancestors. Indeed, emotions such as fear are designed to trigger the stress response (commonly called the "fight-or-flight" response), which mobilizes us to react energetically in emergencies, elevating blood pressure and heart rate and directing blood flow to the large muscles, thus preparing us to stand and fight or run away.

When fight-or-flight works best, we briefly mobilize for the emergency. The system then quickly recovers once the emergency has passed—returning to the baseline state, to what scientists call homeostasis, in which breathing, blood pressure, and so on return to normal. But as the past fifty years of research on stress has demonstrated, sometimes, when fight-or-flight is regularly triggered, the body doesn't return to its baseline state. Rather, it maintains a heightened state of vigilance that can contribute to a number of problems, including fatigue, weight gain, heart disease, and diabetes. As Robert Sapolsky, one of today's main stress researchers, observes, under conditions of chronic activation, "the stress response itself becomes damaging."[7]

Thus how we respond emotionally to the events in our online lives can have real consequences for both our effectiveness and our health. Strong emotions can hijack us, diverting our attention from what we were intending to do (as we saw several times in the scenario in Chapter 2). And the accumulated stress of our difficult emotions can compromise our health and well-being over the long term.

Fortunately, we aren't helpless victims at the mercy of our negative emotions—or needn't be. Unlike our evolutionary ancestors, we don't have to react automatically once strong emotions have been triggered. We can, in principle, bring thought and reflection to bear, pausing long enough to assess the situation and to respond differently. We may not be able to turn off this alerting mechanism, but we can exercise discretion when it triggers us, and make conscious decisions about whether and how to respond to the information it is providing. Just because I find a Facebook post upsetting doesn't mean that I have to respond directly from that emotion—or even respond at all. And I may even be able to reduce the impact of the triggering emotion by refusing to feed it with further negative thoughts ("I can't believe she said that! I never liked her anyway . . . ").

In other words, we can learn to work with our emotions in more constructive ways. (This is the basis of a recent educational movement called social and emotional intelligence.) Emotions don't have to hijack us so often—and when they do, we have the potential to return to a stable emotional state more quickly. Last chapter, we saw how the guilt I felt about avoiding my colleague's email message triggered a new act of avoidance (checking the *New York Times* Web site). This shift of focus happened without any awareness on my part, either of the triggering emotion or the "decision" to shift. But with greater self-awareness, I might have noticed my emotional reaction before it precipitated an un-thinking, automatic reaction. I could then have paused and assessed the situation and decided what to do: whether or not to switch tasks. Thus, although strong emotions can hijack attention, skillful attention paid to these emotions at the time they arise can help us manage them.[8]

The Body's Place in Our Online Lives

Naturally, the state of our bodies is also important to our online lives. To some, this assertion may seem too obvious to mention. But to others, it needs to be stated and defended. For our Cartesian heritage gives primacy to the mind over the body, at times suggesting that the body is at best a necessary evil. Yet recent work in cognitive science challenges this position, asserting that mind and body are a single integrated system, and that the body is necessarily a full participant in all aspects of our lives. Whatever our philosophical position, however, when we go online we often seem to behave as if we were brains on a stick, pretending that we don't have bodies, or at least ignoring the signals our bodies are sending us. No wonder that we suffer a range of body ailments—including carpal tunnel syndrome, neck and back problems, and eyestrain—as well as the more serious stress-related ailments I mentioned above.[9]

While these forms of body discomfort and dysfunction are important in their own right—who wants to live with chronic pain?—they can also affect the quality of our online work. Strong body sensations, much like strong negative emotions, can hijack our attention, making it hard to concentrate. And low-grade, chronic pain can sap our energy, contributing to a fatigue that chips away at wholehearted engagement. (One common response to this, numbing ourselves to the discomfort, prolongs and exacerbates the chronic condition.)

Paying attention to the body can thus alert us to the physical discomfort we've been ignoring, and can allow us to address it. Sometimes it is a matter of shifting positions, or getting up and moving around. (There is increasing evidence that our sedentary lives, much of it now spent in front of our digital devices, can contribute to a range of serious ailments, including obesity, diabetes, and heart disease.) Sometimes, we may want or need to consult health care professionals, or to take up a body-oriented practice such as yoga.[10]

But all this, while true and important enough, makes it sound like the body matters primarily because it can drag us down (a curious expression) if we're not attentive to its aches and pains. There is also a more positive spin on the place of the body. It turns out that we can actually improve our mood and increase the quality of our attention through posture and movement. There is now evidence that exercise—something as simple as going for a walk—can not only lift our mood but strengthen our attention and intelligent engagement with whatever we're doing. And the simple act of smiling can increase positive feelings. So there is little doubt that adopting a relaxed and alert posture while we're sitting in front of our computers, and taking breaks to move around, can increase both our well-being and our effectiveness.[11]

While posture, facial expression, and movement clearly matter, the breath occupies a special place as both an active participant in our current state of being and as a passive reflector of it. Breathing is a fundamental life process, which is closely tied not only to survival but to well-being. When we are relaxed and happy, we tend to breathe slowly and deeply. And when we are stressed out, we often breathe rapidly and shallowly—an indicator that we are experiencing the fight-or-flight response. The breath is thus a fairly reliable indicator of our current state of mind. We may deny, or try to ignore, our emotional state, but checking in with our breath gives us a way to hear what our body has to say about the matter.

What's more, the quality of our breathing not only reflects our state of mind but affects it. Shallow breathing deprives the body of needed oxygen, which may contribute to anxiety and to other psychological and physiological conditions. Something as simple as noticing shallow breathing and taking deeper, more relaxed breaths can serve a restorative function. Linda Stone, a former Apple and Microsoft executive, has written about what she calls "email apnea," pointing to our tendency to hold our breath while doing email. "I predict, within the next five to seven years, breathing exercises will be a significant part of every fitness regime," she says. "In the meantime, why not breathe while doing email?"[12]

Training in Our Digital Craft

In Chapter 1, I suggested we think of our online work as a kind of craft, as a highly skilled set of activities. I likened it to playing a sport or engaging in a handcraft. In each case—whether it's playing baseball or soccer, doing calligraphy or making furniture—there are skills that are specific to that particular craft: how to swing a bat, kick a ball, manipulate a pen, or hold a saw. Equally in our online work, there are many skills that are specific to the digital world: how to use particular hardware devices and different kinds of software, how to communicate appropriately using different social media, and so on. But across all these crafts there are important commonalities. In this chapter we have been exploring some of these: the value in cultivating attention, a balanced emotional state, and a relaxed and attuned body.

The craft perspective also highlights another important feature of our online lives: that we can improve our digital craft through practice and training. Yet I often hear people talking as if they're simply stuck with the skill level they've currently attained. This is especially evident when we complain about our attentional limitations, about how distracted we are. Fortunately, the counterevidence is both definitive and clear: we *can* train ourselves to be more attentive, both online and offline. Earlier I suggested that attention is like a flashlight beam. Another useful metaphor is that it is a kind of muscle. There is a growing body of evidence that this muscle, much like our biceps and abs, can be strengthened through appropriate use.[13]

Strengthening Task Focus

William James suggested that training people in "voluntarily bringing back a wandering attention, over and over again" would be "*the* education *par excellence*" (the emphasis is his). Few of us can sustain our focus on an object with complete, unwavering concentration. But we *can* voluntarily bring our attention back when we notice that we have strayed. And it turns out that the more that we do this, restoring our focus "over and over again," the less often we are likely to wander and the more quickly we will notice when we have. If attention is a muscle, this technique is like doing reps at the gym.[14]

One of the simplest and most widespread forms of attention training uses the breath as the object of focus. You sit (or stand, or lie down), paying attention to your in-breath and out-breath. When the mind wanders (recall that the mind's "default mode" is a kind of inner monologue), you simply bring your focus back to the breath. This practice exercises and strengthens the three attentional skills I have discussed above: focusing, opening (or noticing), and choosing. For your job is to focus on your breath, to notice when you have strayed, and then to choose to come back to the breath, however tempting whatever has distracted you may be.

Appendix A presents a version of this attention training practice, which I call mindful breathing. I realize that some readers will already engage in such a practice—mindful attention to the breath is becoming as common as yoga in our culture—or will at least have tried it. Others may be curious and willing to give it a go, and still others may feel some resistance to it. To this last group I would say the following: You won't actually need to practice mindful breathing in order to perform the exercises in this book. But in some of the exercises you will be bringing your attention back, again and again, to a particular object of focus. (Email or Facebook or texting will be your object of focus in Exercise 2.) In other words, built into some of the exercises is the equivalent of the mindful breathing practice. Why then, you might wonder, do I bother to introduce it at all? First, because it is a simple and useful attention-training exercise that some people love. And second, because even those of you who resist it may find that a stripped-down version of it—which consists in periodically taking a few mindful breaths—is a useful warm-up or retuning exercise, like stretching before going out for a run.

Strengthening Self-Observation/Awareness

While mindful breathing is optional, a second attention-training practice, the mindful check-in, is not. The mindful check-in is a means of increasing your self-awareness. As presented in Appendix A, it asks you to become aware of your attention, your emotions, your breath and body—the very conditions of your immediate experience that we've been discussing in this chapter. (This practice, too, asks you to exercise your focusing, noticing, and choosing skills, although in a somewhat different way than in the mindful breathing practice. You will be noticing certain conditions of your mind and body, and choosing to focus on some of them long enough to observe them in detail.)

You will be making use of the mindful check-in in all the exercises, and if you like, you can wait until you've actually begun the exercises to read through the instructions. But I suggest you read them now and try the practice: How are you feeling right now?

4

Exercise 1

Observing Email (or Facebook or Texting . . .)

My favorite part of this exercise was the level of attention I was giving to my habits. Before paying attention this week, I never really knew what I was doing. I have often described the experience of bouncing mindlessly along the Internet as an "Internet blackout." Thankfully, instead of waking up on a dirty sidewalk with no shoes or money in Las Vegas, I just "wake up" somewhere out there on the Internet. I'll find myself looking at animated gifs of Beyoncé at the Super Bowl, and have NO IDEA how I got there. . . . I am sure that paying attention to my habits is the first step to helping me focus when I need to, and to resist the (deliciously) tempting distractions of the Internet.

—Emily

If I took a second to ask myself, "Why am I checking my email right now?" I would save myself a lot of unnecessary stress and annoyance.

—Vivian

Imagine sending letters at the speed of light. Well into the twentieth century, such a feat was physically impossible, and best left to science fiction to envision. It had taken hundreds of years to create efficient national and transnational postal systems. The best of them could deliver the mail quickly and efficiently. In London in the late nineteenth century, there were multiple pickups and deliveries each day, and it was possible to send a letter and receive a reply the same day. The telegraph, an early-nineteenth-century invention, did in fact allow coded messages to be sent at light speed, but telegrams were costly and usually brief, and you had to go to a centralized place to send and receive them.

So email, invented roughly fifty years ago, was clearly a remarkable step forward. Strictly speaking, email wasn't a digital *letter* (it didn't exactly look like one or behave like one), and its immediate predecessor wasn't actually the letter. Rather, email copied features of the office memo (short for memorandum), which was invented around the turn of the twentieth century as a shortened form of the business letter. In the memo, fields like To, From, and Subject were meant to speed up the delivery and comprehension of office communications, in part by eliminating the flowery openings and closings—such as "yours very truly"—that were the norm in letter writing at the time.[1]

This trend toward abbreviated writing and faster delivery has of course continued since email appeared on the scene. Now we have instant messaging, texting, Twitter, and the like, and these communicative forms can be composed and accessed not only on our personal computers but on our mobile devices. So email is no longer the only means of digital letter writing, as it was for at least the first twenty years of its existence. Nor is it the coolest, the most cutting-edge, as young people have opted for more recently invented modes not yet colonized by their parents and grandparents.

Despite this growing range of choices, email remains a vital communication tool, both for business and for personal exchange. In 2014, there were four billion email accounts worldwide, with the number expected to exceed five billion by the end of 2018. More than 200 billion email messages are now sent every day, roughly 55 percent of which are business oriented. Workers spend a considerable amount of their work time managing email, with estimates as high as 50 percent. And while the use of social media for personal communication is growing rapidly, the amount of email sent for personal exchange is still considerable: nearly 90 billion messages in 2015.[2]

It isn't hard to see why email persists. We use it so extensively, especially in the workplace, because it is the common coin of the realm, because we have a great deal of facility with it that comes from many years of experience, and because it *works.* Yet at the same time, many of us have an uneasy relationship with this form of communication, recognizing it as a source of frustration, stress, overload, and overwork. ("Though it is tremendously useful and will never die," says Farhad Manjoo in the *New York Times,* "email is also, for many people, completely annoying.")[3] Those email messages just keep coming, day and night, announcing upcoming events, inquiring about tasks not yet completed, adding to conversational threads that never seem to end. I've noticed over the years that just catching sight of my email inbox is enough to stress me out.

What exactly is the problem with email? Is it that we receive too many messages to cope with? That we don't have the right management strategy for sorting, responding to, and archiving the wealth of messages we receive? Could the problem be with our particular email client, or our failure to properly understand and use its more advanced features, such as filtering? A little searching online will turn up all these diagnoses and more. Just try doing a search on "email overload" and you will come upon all manner of tools and techniques to help you address some version of the problem.

While many of these tools and techniques are, or can be, quite useful, adopting them unreflectively puts the cart before the horse—or, more precisely, the treatment before the diagnosis. Surely, there is no single right way to solve everyone's email problems. We are all different: our jobs are different, our cognitive capacities are different, and so is our emotional makeup. But if we pay more attention to what happens when we use email and how it makes us feel, we will have more of a basis for diagnosing the problem, *our* problem, and for doing something about it.

In my classes, the first exercise I assign is the email observation exercise, and I present the exercise to my students much as I am about to do here. I choose email over, say, Facebook, Twitter, or some other social media application both because it remains a significant part of our collective lives and because it is the only communication tool that everyone in the class is guaranteed to use. Young students, who mainly use other media for personal communication, must have and use email accounts, since official university life depends upon it. Besides, once they enter the workforce, they will discover how important email remains. And older, returning students or working professionals are totally immersed in email, and many express frustration with it.

But you needn't select email as your object of study in this first exercise. You are free to choose Facebook or Twitter or texting, or

any other single application. It should be straightforward to substitute
Facebook (say), for email, and to make the other changes this substitu-
tion requires. But if you are doing this exercise with others, I strongly
recommend that you all choose the same application, so you can easily
compare notes with one another.

Overview of the Email Observation Exercise

Each of us handles email somewhat differently. Some of us check email
on our computers, while others of us mainly use our phones. Still others use a combination of devices. Some of us have email open and available all day long, reading and responding to messages as soon as they
arrive, while others restrict themselves to a limited number of email
sessions per day. Some of us maintain separate accounts for business,
family, and friends, while others funnel all their mail through one primary account. This exercise asks you to pay attention to your current
email strategy: to the habits that you've formed, whether consciously
or unconsciously, around how you read and write email messages, and
around how you manage your inbox.

But the exercise also asks you to notice how you *feel* when you perform these operations. What emotions arise when you first catch sight
of your inbox, or when you see certain messages there? What effects do
these emotions have on you (on your body posture, on your breathing,
on your thinking)? What do these reactions lead you to do? And how
effective are these habitual ways of reacting, when you honestly reflect
on them? Might you make other choices—develop a somewhat different strategy for handling email—once you begin to see your current
habits?

Box 4.1: The Email Observation Exercise

What to do

Use email as you normally do, paying attention both to the email activities you are performing and to what you are experiencing in your mind and body as you perform them. Use this information to notice your habitual patterns of behavior, what motivates them, and how these patterns affect your effectiveness and well-being. Make changes, based on your discoveries, and formulate them as personal guidelines.

Why do it?

• To practice (and strengthen) your ability to observe yourself.

• To use the information gathered from self-observation to improve your email craft.

Few of us, of course, tend to bring this level of self-observation and awareness to our online activity. We get into a kind of *doing mode,* where we're mainly focused on results, on what we're trying to make happen next. When there are gaps in this stream of activity, because we're waiting for a system or a person to respond, we'll often switch to another task and continue doing something else. Or we'll wait impatiently and distractedly for a response. We're generally not very present to what we're feeling or experiencing in the moment. But now, in this first exercise, you will be able to see that the mind and body provide a vantage point, an observation station, from which to observe and reflect upon the character and quality of your online activities, and that this kind of seeing can lead to insights that will enhance what you do.

How to Do the Email Observation Exercise

Box 4.2 summarizes the six steps in the exercise, as I introduced them in Chapter 2. Let's work through each of them in turn.

Step 1: Perform the primary practice (do email)

The heart of the exercise is simple and straightforward: just do your email. For twenty minutes or half an hour, pay attention to your inbox (or to multiple inboxes, if you prefer). Scan your inbox. Open and read messages. Reply to some of them. Compose new messages. Do exactly what you would normally do at this time and place. Do this "primary practice" once a day for several days, or preferably for an entire week.

As you perform these activities, I ask you just to pay attention to your email. But I realize that not everyone normally works with their email as a solo activity. Some of us prefer to multitask when we use email, switching between email and other apps. And some of us don't even think of email as a discrete activity (we don't do email in "sessions"). If these descriptions apply to you, you have two choices: For the period devoted to this exercise, you can limit yourself just to email, artificial though this may feel. Or, you can maintain your normal multitasking behavior, but focus your attention primarily on your email.

Box 4.2: The Steps of the Email Observation Exercise

Step 1: Perform the primary practice (do email)
Conduct one or more email sessions as you normally would do.

Step 2: Observe what you are doing and feeling
Pay attention both to the email activities you are performing (reading and writing email messages, scanning your inbox, etc.) and to what you are feeling (what is happening in or to your breath and body, your thoughts and emotions, your attentional focus) as you perform these activities.

Step 3: Log what you are observing
Keep a running record of what you observe in Step 2.

Step 4: Consolidate (summarize) your observations
Review your log, looking for larger patterns. How do you habitually react to certain email events? How effective are these patterns?

Step 5: Formulate personal guidelines
What do these patterns suggest about how to use email in healthier and more effective ways?

Step 6: Share and discuss
Talk with others about what you've been discovering.

Step 2: Observe what you are doing and feeling

While you are using email, you should also pay attention to what you are experiencing as you use it. The mindful check-in (first described in Chapter 3 and more fully explained in Appendix A) guides you to notice what is happening in your mind and body—the quality of your attention, your emotional state, the state of your breath and body—while you are on email. Observing in this way will give you the chance to identify bottlenecks, points of constriction, in your email practice, as well as places where your efforts are easy and free-flowing. Identifying such places allows you to ask, "What is going on here? What does this tell me about the way I currently use email?"

Step 3: Log what you are observing

This next step consists in logging (taking notes on) what you have been observing, as preparation for step 4, where you will be consolidating and summarizing what you've observed. I suggest that you maintain a written log, either digitally or on paper, where you jot down observations as they arise—or shortly after the primary practice is over, if you prefer. (Appendix B gives you a possible format for your log.)

So what exactly should you record? I suggest that you note the date and time you began observing and the time you stopped. You might also note the current environment in which you're performing the exercise. (Are you at home, on the bus, sitting in a noisy coffee house?) Then you will want to note specifically what was happening and how it made you feel. Are you suddenly aware that you've been holding your

breath? What were you doing at that moment, and what does this tell
you? Do you now notice that you feel relaxed and content? How is this
related to what you've just been doing or thinking?

These are all the instructions I generally offer about logging in my
course. In practice, I find that students log whatever is most salient
and at whatever level of detail is most useful to them. But to give you a
feeling for the range of possible log entries, here are three actual entries
written by my students:

> Breathing . . . wow, I'm just about holding my breath just looking
> at the inbox tab. Body is a bit strained, stiff, head a little forward,
> arms are tight, not relaxed at all; my knees are tightly crossed and
> my lower back is a bit achy. Mood: resentful as though I don't
> have a choice whether to check email or not, feels like an inter-
> ruption to other projects that are more to my liking.
>
> —*Holly*

> My body and mind were all over the place during this email ses-
> sion. . . . I opened my laptop to an inbox of fifteen emails, all of
> which seemed important. As I scanned the list for signs of junk or
> easy answers, I resolved those few, then decided to get up and go
> get some water. I came back and decided to read each email and
> turn it into a to-do on my list next to the computer. I started to
> notice my fatigue from working out over the weekend, and spent
> most of the reading time leaning on one elbow. When I moved
> it out of the way to start responding, I felt more awake because
> I was sitting up, but it was a challenge to combat the muscle

soreness. However, the challenges I was dealing with in my emails overtook my physical awareness and I only noticed my fatigue when I finally stood up to go to a meeting.

—Barry

On computer, on couch, leaned forward (just head, back leaned back). Listening to roommate talk . . . absentmindedly opening email, seeing nothing new, closing it and then opening again out of habit . . . little or no engagement. Hardly even realizing what I'm doing!

—Doug

Step 4: Consolidate (summarize) your observations

Now read through your notes and reflect on them. You might think that this step is unnecessary, but it's actually quite important. The entries in your log are likely to be fairly raw and terse, and specific to the moment. Looking back over everything you've written will give you the chance to notice patterns that may not have been obvious in the moment, and to fill out your understanding by comparing and contrasting multiple observations. Are there times when you use email as a distraction from other more important activities? Why do you check email when you do, and how well does this work for you? Does it make a difference whether you are checking email on your computer or on your phone?

This is where paying attention to your immediate experience can really pay off. When your email practice is problematic (whatever that means for you), you may find that you've been holding your breath, or collapsing your chest, or feeling anxious or upset. And when your email practice is going well, you may find indications of that in your mind and body—a greater sense of relaxation, a lightness of mood.

I also suggest that you write about the patterns you are discovering. This can serve two useful purposes. First, it can help you clarify your thoughts, as writing and journaling often do. And second, it will give you valuable material to share with others in Step 6 below. Box 4.3 provides some questions to help you organize your thinking and writing.

Step 5: Formulate personal guidelines

The summary remarks that you've just created will give you a good sense of what's currently working well and what isn't. This understanding provides the basis for making useful changes, which you should now formulate as personal guidelines for future behavior. But let me stress that these guidelines are *personal:* They are particular to your observations and habits. They don't need to work for anyone else. What's more, they are *provisional:* subject to further change as you discover more about yourself, or as your circumstances change.

Broadly speaking, there are two kinds of changes you might consider making: to your online practices (to what you do) and to yourself (to how you are). When you see changes you can make that will improve your effectiveness—for example, by reducing the amount of email you have to deal with or by limiting the number of times you check email during the day—then by all means make them. In this instance, you might write a guideline that says "empty my inbox at the end of each day," or "deal with email no more than three times a day." (Some people find that techniques like Inbox Zero can be of help, as well as software that limits which apps they can access.)

Box 4.3: Noticing Patterns in Your Email Behavior

1. What did you do?
How many sessions did you observe? For how long? During these sessions, did you work exclusively on email, or did you interleave other tasks at the same time? Was this your normal mode of behavior?

2. In observing breath, body/posture, emotions, and attention, which of these dimensions of your present experience were most salient?
What did they reveal to you about how you currently use email (about what's working well and what isn't)? Did you notice any of these aspects of your mind and body changing over the course of a session? In what ways and on what basis?

3. Were you able to notice the impulse to check email?
What was going on in your mind and body at that moment? What does this tell you about when and why you check email?

4. Were you able to notice the state of your mind and body when you first laid eyes on your inbox?
What does this tell you?

> 5. *While you were using email, did you notice the impulse to switch to some other task?*
> Did you switch (sometimes, always, never)? What does this suggest about your current online behaviors/habits?
>
> 6. *Summarize what you learned from the exercise*
> Talk with others about what you've been discovering.

But if you find that you can't change the external conditions—because, for example, your job requires you to be online and continuously handling a torrent of email messages—you still have the possibility of changing the way you deal with these circumstances *inside yourself*. Thus noticing the resistance you feel to handling all this email and how it affects your body and your emotions, you might decide to reduce your stress by acknowledging what you're feeling and making a conscious effort to relax in the face of the torrent.

And while you're carefully noticing constrictions and bottlenecks in your current practice, don't ignore those aspects that are currently working well. Those times when you are relaxed, attentive, and effective—when your actions are easy and free-flowing—can also be a source of useful information and guidance. One of my students, a doctoral student named Jonathan, was surprised to see how good email actually made him feel, and while many of his classmates were deciding to limit their use of it, he realized that he needed to maintain his current level of use, and possibly even increase it.

Step 6: Share and discuss

At this point, you will have three written sources of insight: a log of your observations, a consolidation of your log entries that summarizes your main discoveries, and a set of personal guidelines that express the changes you intend to make. In this final step, I strongly urge you to share with others what you've been learning, showing them your summary and guidelines and discussing the discoveries contained in them.

This kind of sharing is an essential element in my classes and workshops. And it is something the students greatly enjoy. It gives people the chance to compare their experiences with those of others, and to learn about patterns of behavior that they themselves may want to investigate. It also reveals the diversity in their online practices, and illustrates, in a visceral and concrete way, that no single set of rules will ever work for everyone. The back-and-forth discussion that's provoked by these conversations becomes an additional source of clarification and learning.

If you are reading this book with others, as part of a workplace study group or a community reading group, I urge you to exchange your written remarks with one another and to take the time to discuss them. And if you are doing the exercises alone, I still suggest you find a way to share your insights with others. (You might blog about them, for example.) But if you are determined not to write up what you have been learning, consider having a conversation with a friend or a coworker, even if he or she hasn't done the exercise. Your discussion with an interested listener will further your own thinking, and it may stimulate your dialogue partner to undertake the exercise for him- or herself.

What Others Report

Now that you've performed the email observation exercise (or at least read through it), I want to give you a feeling for the kinds of discoveries that other people make.

The Emotional Dimension of Email

One of the first and most common discoveries is that email is a very emotional business. On the face of it, this may not seem like much of an insight. Most of us already know that we have strong reactions to email. Indeed, many of us express some level of frustration with it. But in paying greater attention to their moment-to-moment experience, people regularly express surprise at the depth and extent of their emotional reactions. Often they characterize these reactions in highly negative terms, using words like "anxiety," "dissatisfaction," "dread," "worry," and "repulsion." But not all reports are negative: people also notice depths of positive emotion that they weren't previously aware of, including the satisfaction of completing something or the joy of being in touch with loved ones.

In my experience, however, negative emotions do seem to predominate. It isn't hard to understand why. The amount of email we have to deal with, the fact that it's never ending and we rarely feel caught up—these can obviously trigger bad feelings. Then too, specific email messages may provoke strong emotions, some because they involve deliverables and deadlines, others because they are expressions of other people's bad moods, or because they come from people with whom we have complex relationships. If you look closely, you may notice that every message (and the task it's associated with) carries a certain emotional charge. And as a result, simply scanning a couple of vertical inches of your inbox may give you a case of emotional whiplash. Will, a middle-aged manager, has described this as "getting flipped back and forth between twenty thoughts." "It's not a great experience," he adds.

Why is it useful to see the strong emotional dimension of our email use? For one thing, just seeing it clearly can stimulate us to do something about it, even before we know what that might entail. But beyond just showing us the extent of the problem, noticing strong emotions can point us to specific pressure points and bottlenecks. And this can lead us to make specific changes that will reduce our bad feelings: If the amount of email in our inbox is a major emotional trigger, then adopting a zero inbox policy may be a good solution. If we discover that reading email just before going to bed is a source of aggravation, making it harder to fall sleep, then maybe we should stop doing it.

One of the most common discoveries is that strong emotions can trigger us to check email more often than is useful or healthy. Sometimes, it's the hope that we'll find something special waiting for us, a hope that is rarely fulfilled. As Vivian, an undergraduate, comments, "The reason I feel the need to check my email all the time on my phone is the hope that I will have a new message from one or two people that I would love to hear from. But the fact is that 90+ percent of the time my emails are not of that personal nature. . . . I am always hoping it will be the email I have been waiting for." Others notice that email is a way to get away from unpleasant feelings, or to procrastinate, as Anne, a master's student, observes: "I most often feel the urge [to check email] when I would rather be doing something else. The most common time is during work. I use email checking as an excuse to defer the unpleasant and unstimulating task of doing my job."

Just seeing this behavior and how it controls us can suggest alternative responses. "If I took a second to ask myself, 'Why am I checking my email right now?'" Vivian wrote, "I would save myself a lot of unnecessary stress and annoyance." The following guideline, written by Maria, a master's student in her early twenties, is a fairly typical response to this problem: "Avoid the impulse to check email numerous times a day. Whenever I feel the urge to check email out of the blue, engage in a healthy activity like reading, taking a walk, biking, etc."

But there isn't a single right answer to this problem. Someone might decide that frequent email checking out of anxiety or boredom was actually a valuable strategy and simply continue doing it. (Perhaps it does momentarily alleviate your negative state. Or perhaps you simply accept it as one of your little quirks.) This exercise isn't about following general rules imposed from elsewhere, or adopting a practice because the internalized voice of your mother or your partner tells you that you "should" do it. Rather, it's about discovering what works for you.

The Importance of Breath and Body

Just as people are surprised by the amount of emotion they're feeling while they're using email, they are often surprised at how unaware they were of their bodies. Deborah, a Web developer in her late thirties, noticed that it wasn't hard for her to tune in to her thoughts and emotions while she was doing email, but paying attention to physical sensations was a different matter. "I generally don't think that I need my body when I'm composing an email," she says, realizing how laughable this sounds. "Of course we need our bodies! I think that I've become so used to the pain I have in my hands, wrists, neck, shoulders and back that I have learned to desensitize myself so that I might continue working. This is a disturbing realization for me." This discovery led her to remember the last job she'd had where she had more physical mobility, when she worked as a waitress. Certainly it had its problems, but "the variety of movement resulted in more energy overall." And thus she resolved to integrate more movement into her daily routine, including standing, short walks, and stretching.

Some come to see how important the breath is, both as a diagnostic tool and as a means of improving their relationship with email. "In reviewing my email observations," says Kathy, a mother of two adult children, "it's clear that I suffer from stress virtually each and every time I open my email. . . . When I am stressed, I hold my breath or breathe in a shallow way." Having seen this, she realizes what she needs to do. "If I change nothing else, I think it's important that I unlearn this reflex. Breathing more deeply creates calm and eases anxiety." And Nichola, an undergraduate planning to work in the tech industry, comes to a similar understanding, expressing it as a personal guideline: "Take five deep breaths before opening my inbox. This will help me to check in with my body and hopefully become more aware of how my inner state affects how I see the world (and email)."

Paying Attention to Attention

When asked to observe their attention, some people notice how distracted they typically are. "When checking email," Maria comments,

"I notice many voices and images in my head. I think about assignments due, meals I need to cook, people I need to call and meet up with, bills I need to pay, and the pain of my recent break-up." And Krista, who works in an art gallery, notes that email takes her out of the present moment. "While I am doing it, I feel neither alert nor relaxed. I lose all sense of time, physicality, and emotions. It is only after I finish email, that I come to my senses."

Others, however, discover and are surprised by how attentive they actually are: "The quality of my attention to my email is very high," says Ashley, who is working toward a graduate library degree. "When I am actively reading or responding to messages, I am perhaps the most intensely focused of any activity throughout my whole day. I am more able to shut out distractions while doing email than while reading or engaged in conversation."

Still others notice that the quality of their attention varies considerably, depending on a variety of factors. Some are more attentive when they're using email on their computer, while others find that their focus is stronger when they're using their smart phone. Some find that their depth of concentration varies with the type of message they are dealing with. Others notice that their degree of concentration depends on the time of day. One woman, a computer consultant named Heather, came to see that she was much more focused, and therefore more effective, while doing email in the morning. "In the morning," she noted, "I am taking a purposeful swim in my inbox, getting a couple good healthy laps in. In the afternoon, I am being pushed in the pool with my clothes on."

Having seen when they are at times more and less attentive, and having observed how their quality of attention supports or obstructs their goals, people are then in a position to make changes. Having noticed "many voices and images in my head," Maria decided that it really mattered to her to be more focused. "This email exercise has taught me how cluttered my mind is and how it really disables me from truly being present with the task at hand." And she committed to treating email "like meditation," as an activity in which she could cultivate and practice a deeper form of concentration. (We will explore this possibility further in the next chapter.)

And Heather, who found herself pushed into the pool during her afternoon email sessions, decided to make two changes. One was to see if she could modify her afternoon behavior to learn from, and to mimic, her morning behavior. The other was to reserve her morning time for the email activities that required the greatest focus. She wrote a personal guideline that read: "Consistently use your morning session, that time when you are most calm and organized, to clear and label your inbox. Resolve any messages that you can immediately so they don't sit around and cause undue stress or anxiety."

Our Overall Relationship with Email

As these examples show, the email observation exercise can help us observe and make changes to specific behaviors. But it can also reveal aspects of our overall relationship to email: What is our basic attitude toward email? How do we treat it, and how does it treat us?

Ashley talks about her inbox as a being she has a real relationship with: "Emotionally, I feel a kind of responsibility to my email inbox, as if it requires tending to survive and remain vital, like a plant that needs water or a relationship that needs time and attention. I also go to it with emotional expectations: to be distracted, redirected, renewed;

to reward myself for doing something else that required a lot of focus or was tedious; to remind myself of who I am in some way; to feel in touch with others; to feel needed and valued; or to feel in control of my time."

Others describe their relationship with email in more negative terms. Holly, who works at a community college, discovered that she feels like "a dog being wagged by its email tail. Until actually keeping a log and then analyzing it, I was mostly unaware or unconscious of just how much my email controls and affects me both mentally and physically. It's as though my email is there every day, lurking in the corners of my mind and whispering, 'You know you'll have to check me sooner or later—you'll have to stop whatever it is that you're doing and deal with me, your inbox.' I was aware of my consistent reluctance to check email, but never actually looked into why that is or how to fix it."

If this is how you view your email, then no wonder it's so stressful. The first step in changing our relationship is recognizing it for what it is. All of these people were able to see how their uncomfortable relationship with email was coloring their uses of it—how it was allowing email to control *them*. And all of them were then able to rethink and rework their uses of email in concrete ways to establish a more congenial relationship. Lydia, a graphic artist, reports that "email is not the enemy. It is just the messenger that reminds you about your enemy: Stop being afraid that the inbox is a 24/7 scroll of bad news. It is not. There are plenty of emails that are helpful, instructional, positive, and some are full of love. For two weeks, I have programmed pleasant emails to arrive in my inbox from another account."

But some people conclude that email itself isn't actually the problem at all. Rick, retired from a government job, realized that his problems with email "are life problems, the ones that predate comput-ers, the ones that are part of being a human being. They are the prob-lems I have with people or situations or my own perceptions of myself and the world. The emails that create stress or unpleasant feelings are the ones that deal with my obligations to others or myself. I could de-lete all of my email accounts and these problems will still be there."

For such people, in other words, what matters most isn't their rela-tionship *with* email, but the relationships they cultivate *through* email. This suggests that we pay attention to our deeper intentions when we're using email. What is the quality of the relationships we want to cultivate?

Final Reflections

Rick's observation points to the fact that email is actually more than email. For email is a medium of communication, a major instrument for managing our tasks and relationships. And this means that many of the problems we associate with it come from the challenging nature of our lives: figuring out how to work and play well with others, how to manage the unavoidable stresses of living a human life. And what this means is that not all our email problems can be addressed alone, or by making adjustments to the technology. Some changes will require social intervention—for example, by establishing new norms or social agreements within our work group, among our family members, or within our network of friends. And some changes may need to be made at a societal level—in the way we think about work and play, about time together and time apart.

In a 2010 journal article entitled "Email as a Source and Symbol of Stress," Stephen R. Barley, a professor in the Department of Management Science and Engineering at Stanford, and two colleagues report on a study of email use they conducted at a major high tech corporation. They were interested in understanding how the various communication technologies employees use affected their level of stress. And so they collected data on the way employees communicated in face-to-face meetings, email sessions, voicemail sessions, phone calls and teleconferences, instant messaging, and so on. They discovered, of course, that *all* these communication modes were stressful in a variety of ways.

But they also discovered that email was different in one significant and intriguing way: Email was the mode that people complained about the most. In trying to understand why, they concluded that email was the most visible sign of people's sense of overwork. Whereas a teleconference or a face-to-face meeting had a beginning and an end, everyone knew that email was always on, and even when they were sleeping new email was accumulating in their inboxes. If they wanted to see, literally and figuratively, the demands of their jobs, they had only to look at their inboxes. This suggested to Barley and his collaborators that email wasn't the problem—or, more accurately, that it was only part of the problem. For email was in fact more than email—it was the most visible symbol of people's endless work and therefore an easy scapegoat for their complaints.

To the extent that we fail to understand this, Barley and his colleagues conclude, "employees and organizations are unlikely to recognize and address the larger problem: new patterns of work that crowd days and create unrealistic expectations about response time. To the degree that email's symbolic force diverts attention from the stress created by the demands being placed on a downsized and globalized workforce, it serves as a red herring." While I believe this is right, I am convinced that each of us can, and should, bring greater balance to our own individual practice.

5

Exercise 2

Focused Email (or Facebook or Texting . . .)

I learned that going into a task with a high level of focus does wonders for accomplishing things. I don't think I have ever gotten so much email accomplished and felt so successful before than while doing this assignment.

—Eric

Telling myself to focus on email actually helped make the process less stressful. I had permission to let go of things because it was time for email and email only. Focusing on one thing is less stressful than panicking about fifty.

—Emily

In performing the email observation exercise, Maria got a good look at just how distracted she typically was when using email. In addition to noticing the many voices and images in her head, she saw that she was usually checking other information sources, especially Facebook, at the same time she was on email. "It's like Facebook is a part of my daily life," she commented, "which is why I usually open up a Facebook tab when I check my email. Unfortunately, I am usually more invested in Facebook than I am in email. . . . Sometimes I have Facebook opened on both my laptop and my smartphone. In situations like this, I noticed that I am looking for pleasure, instant gratification, and to a large extent, distraction. I find that I waste lots of time browsing Facebook when I should be paying close attention to my email."

Maria found these realizations quite upsetting. But she went a step beyond just observing and feeling bad about her regular state of distraction: She came up with a way to address it. Maybe, she thought, I can work on being more focused when I'm using email. So she tried an experiment: "In checking email, I made an effort to remain conscious of my breathing and to focus my eyes and mind on the task at hand. I checked only emails that pertained to work, education, and employment. I did not want to allow myself to become distracted by random things like Facebook articles, newsfeeds, or distracting thoughts about my recent break-up."

Although it was initially hard for her to focus in this way, it was clearly a revelation. "Through this activity I discovered the power of concentration. Concentration is an act that requires active filtering and decision making. It requires being constantly aware of my physical and mental being. To build a strong state of concentration, I checked one email at a time, thoroughly reading the content and replying. I realized that in order to be completely engaged with my emails, I had to slow down."

Experimenting in this way, she also noticed what might derail her. "Certain messages can trigger emotions that lead to thoughts of the past and future. Additionally, checking email requires one to be plugged in with the digital world. At any moment, one can decide to explore multiple Web sites while chatting, Facebooking, and checking email. This exercise forced me to reflect on ways in which I can challenge myself to live in the present and therefore improve my ability to focus."

In this chapter, you will have the opportunity to explore what Maria discovered: the possibility of engaging with email in a more focused way. The idea is to take your email practice seriously as a craft, and to care enough about what you are reading and writing that you are, in a sense, like the batter at the plate or the woodworker at the bench.

But before we begin to investigate this mode of online behavior I want to be clear about two things. The first is that focusing the mind is hard. Our minds have a natural tendency to wander. We all have the ability to direct our attention to one thing or another, but *keeping it* on a particular object of focus generally requires training. This exercise is likely to show you (as the previous exercise may already have done) how much your mind actually does wander. Fortunately, the more you practice at focusing, the better you will become.

Second, unlike the email observation exercise, this exercise is prescriptive. In the earlier exercise, I gave you a structured practice for noticing your online habits and tendencies, but I didn't tell you what you would find or what changes you should make. Here, however, I *am* telling you what to do. But I'm not saying that you should necessarily adopt this practice as your normal mode of operation from now on. This exercise is an experiment, and when you're done with it you can decide whether to adopt it, whether to selectively incorporate certain aspects of it into your normal routine, or whether to let go of the whole thing. Whatever you ultimately decide, I think you'll find that it has taught you some valuable lessons about your online behavior.

As in the previous exercise, you are welcome to choose a different application as your object of study—Facebook or texting, for example, instead of email. Indeed, if you chose to observe something other than

---

Box 5.1: The Focused Email Exercise

What to do

Do email and only email. When you notice the impulse to stray to some other app (or if you discover that you have already strayed elsewhere), come back to your email.

Why do it?

    • To practice (and strengthen) your ability to maintain task focus.

    • To discover which triggers (internal and external events) typically distract you from your task focus.

    • To discover what actions and conditions help you to stay focused.

    • To decide whether you will want to adopt this approach to email, and if so, when.

---

email in the previous chapter, I recommend that you stick with that same application in this chapter.

Overview of the Focused Email Exercise

At heart this exercise is quite simple. You will need to set aside some dedicated time on one or more days to perform the primary practice—using email, and *only email*. Inevitably, you will notice distractions that tempt you to switch to something else. But in the face of these potential distractors, you will simply return your focus to your email. You may also find yourself acting on the temptation to switch, perhaps without conscious awareness. But when you notice that you've strayed, you will simply come back to your email—as many times as necessary.

Here is an entry from Holly's log, which nicely illustrates the practice of coming back, again and again:

> Got comfortable on the couch with my laptop—not slouching, legs supported & not crossed. Clicked the inbox to twenty-eight emails. . . . The radio in the other room was annoying and distracting—I asked my husband's permission to please turn it down & he did. BACK. Continued reading & processing emails but in less than one minute, our house rabbit jumped up on the couch and I began half-consciously petting the rabbit. BACK. Resumed reading email when I found myself thinking about my daughter's departure . . . and picturing her being weary while driving from the airport to her home. . . . BACK. Began to focus on a response to one of the emails when I realized I was brushing rabbit hair off the seat cover. BACK. Resumed thinking about what I wanted to convey in my email message when I found myself thinking about a nonevent at work this morning. BACK. Got through almost all of the email satisfactorily but realized that I had to pull myself back from both internal and external triggers about fifteen times in a thirty-five-minute period.

I love this description. It is rich with detail, showing how Holly's email session was regularly interrupted both by internal distractions (thoughts about her daughter, about work) and external distractions (the radio, the rabbit). I also love the touch of lightheartedness in her account as she exhorts herself to come BACK, again and again. In light of the challenges this exercise presents, maintaining some curiosity and humor about it isn't such a bad idea.

This exercise can be useful in at least three ways. First, doing it on a regular basis will strengthen your attention so you're more able to stay focused when you want or need to. It does get easier with practice. (In Chapter 3 I likened this to doing reps at the gym to strengthen your muscles.) Second, staying more focused on the task at hand is likely to increase your effectiveness (something, of course, you'll have to verify for yourself). And third, the *attempt* to stay focused in this way will likely show you what tends to pull you away—the various internal and external triggers that exert the greatest influence on you. You will therefore learn more about what normally distracts you, and this can help you remove, or at least anticipate, some of these distractions in the future.

How to Do the Focused Email Exercise

Box 5.2 summarizes the six steps in the exercise.

Step 1: Perform the primary practice (do email exclusively)

As in the email observation exercise, plan to conduct the focused email exercise for one or more sessions. Each session should last for at least fifteen or twenty minutes. I've already explained the essence of the

Box 5.2: The Steps of the Focused Email Exercise

Step 1: Perform the primary practice (do email exclusively)
Do email, and only email. Come back to your email whenever you wander away.

Step 2: Observe what you are doing and feeling
Notice how well you are able to stay focused. Notice when you stray, or when you're tempted to stray. What was happening, and what were you feeling, at those moments?

Step 3: Log what you are observing
Keep a running record of what you observe.

Step 4: Consolidate (summarize) your observations
Review your log, looking for larger patterns. What helps you stay focused? What typically tempts you to stray?

Step 5: Formulate personal guidelines
What do these patterns suggest about how to use email in healthier and more effective ways?

Step 6: Share and discuss
Talk with others about what you've been discovering.

exercise above: Just handle your email to the exclusion of all other online and offline activities. And measure your success not by whether
your focus is unwavering (a nearly impossible goal), but by your willingness to keep bringing your attention back.

Let me also offer you a variant on this exercise. The version I've
explained thus far might be called the restricted version: All activities
outside of your primary practice, email, are forbidden. But there are
times when you might actually switch to another task or application
while still maintaining your intention not to stray. Many of us, for example, regularly make entries in our calendar or our to-do list while
we're reading email. Doing this is actually part of our email practice,
and not doing it can seem awkward and unnatural. If you're one of
these people, you might consider doing a slightly more expansive version of the exercise, in which you allow yourself occasional excursions,
so long as they are directly related to the email activity you're currently
doing. The danger is that seeing your calendar or your to-do list will
distract you from what you were just doing on email. In other words,
it's possible to use your calendar and to-do list in the spirit of this
exercise—but it's also possible to use them to violate, and thus gut, the
exercise. In which case, why do it?

Finally, one of the most basic, and common, forms of attention
training consists in bringing one's attention back, again and again, to
a chosen object of focus. I introduced the mindful breathing practice
(further explained in Appendix A) as one of the most common forms
of such training. While you needn't perform mindful breathing here
(or anywhere in the book, for that matter), some people do find it a
helpful preparation for this exercise. Before starting the exercise, take
a few mindful breaths, or sit for ten or fifteen minutes paying attention

to your breathing, to help settle yourself. You might think of it as a warm-up exercise, like stretching before going for a run.

Step 2: Observe what you are doing and feeling

So what happens when you try to stay focused exclusively on your email? It's likely that you are tempted to stray (like Maria, who found the pull of Facebook hard to resist). Pay attention to what distracts you, as Holly does in the log entry I quoted above. Some of these triggers will be external in nature: Your phone starts ringing, you hear a beep signaling the arrival of a text message, someone knocks on your door. Other triggers arise from internal conditions: You suddenly remember another item for your to-do list, you begin to feel anxious or restless. Performing the mindful check-in (Appendix A) at such moments may help you clarify what you're feeling and how it may be motivating you.

Of course, just as it's hard to stay focused, it can be hard to bring this level of self-observation to bear. You may not be able to notice triggers before you've reacted to them, before you've shifted your focus to something other than email. Or you may be able to do it only occasionally.

Step 3: Log what you are observing

Keep a written record of your observations, at whatever level of detail you find most helpful. (Holly's log entry, which I quote from above, is unusually detailed. Don't feel you need to emulate her.) Here are two more examples:

I am sitting up at my home desk. I have kept my phone on, but faced it down and set it out of my reach. I have an ache in my lower back and my left ankle hurts. I also realize that I had been squinting/furrowing my brow while working on my reflection just moments before. I do this when I concentrate, and it makes my forehead ache. I take a couple of deep breaths and try to consciously loosen the muscles in my face. I start by opening only my personal account. I have no new messages.

—*Susan*

My first session on email and I didn't do too well. I found that I was easily distracted and even though I had the idea to stay focused on the task, I quickly drifted to Facebook or other Web sites at the slightest hint of a divergent thought or task remembrance. The impulse felt reflexive. I cut this session short at around six minutes, but really I didn't follow the guidelines of the exercise at all.

—*Martin*

Step 4: Consolidate (summarize) your observations

Now read through your log, looking for larger patterns. Were there times when it was easier to stay focused on your email? What conditions helped you to do so—changes to your breathing, to your posture, to your immediate environment? Did you make any changes in the way you used email that you found helpful? When did your mind tend to wander? Which triggers, internal or external, tended to exert the most influence on you? Which ones were easy to surmount and which ones were almost impossible to resist? Did you notice any change in your response to triggers as you conducted more sessions?

Write about the patterns you have been discovering. Box 5.3 provides some questions that may help you focus your reflection.

Step 5: Formulate personal guidelines

Finally, based on what you've discovered, formulate personal guidelines that will help you in your future dealings with email. But as you do this, let me remind you of what I said at the beginning of the chapter: While this exercise is prescriptive, my intent isn't to persuade you to adopt this practice all the time. Rather, it's to show you that there is a mode of operating online that is more focused (and potentially healthier and more effective) than what many of us do, and that can be *learned.* Is this practice valuable enough to you to adopt at certain points during the day, and to keep practicing as a way of getting better at it?

If your answer is yes, then when will you decide to practice it? At certain times of the day? When you're trying to accomplish certain tasks? What conditions, internal and external, will help you do your best? If your answer is no, you don't see yourself adopting this practice, *ever,* what have you learned that will be useful to you nonetheless?

Step 6: Share and discuss

How do your reactions to the exercise compare with those of others? It can be fascinating to discover the similarities and differences among your friends and coworkers, and also to sharpen your understanding of

Box 5.3: Noticing Patterns in the Focused Email Exercise

1. What did you do?
How many sessions did you practice the focused email exercise? For how long? Did you do the more or less restricted version? How was this mode of doing email similar to or different from your normal mode?

2. Overall, what was your experience of the exercise?
Was it hard to keep your attention focused on your email? To what extent were you successful?

3. What helped you stay focused?
Did certain conditions, whether internal or external, make it easier for you to stay with your email?

4. What internal and external triggers did you notice?
Which were easiest and which were hardest to deal with?

5. Do you intend to adopt this strategy in the future?
Why or why not? Would you consider adopting it at times, and if so, when?

6. Summarize what you learned from the exercise
What did it show you about your current relationship with email, and how might this affect what you do in the future?

your own tendencies in conversation with them. In the next section, I describe some of the patterns I've observed in teaching my course.

What Others Report

Reactions to the Exercise

Some people actually find the exercise quite easy. They discover that it's liberating, a breath of fresh air, just to focus on email. Erin, a musician, says: "I appreciated the space that focusing on my email for twenty minutes gave me. I felt relaxed and free—not pressed for time or rushing through anything." Some say they've been given "permission" to do just one thing, and to let go, for the moment, of the multiple things crowding in upon them.

Of course, not everyone finds the exercise easy, or pleasant. It can be uncomfortable to discover that much of the time we can't actually control our attention, we can't simply will ourselves to stay on task. It helps to remember that persevering with the exercise leads to improvement.

Discovering the Benefits

Why approach email in this way? Some people see that they're more effective when they're able to more fully concentrate on what they're doing. Jordan, a marketing manager, draws an analogy to splitting firewood: "Each next log demands complete attention and focus, and each swing demands the right level of commitment. I can think of email in a similar way. Each next email is like a new log that needs complete focus and then just the right amount of commitment." (Notice the craft perspective here.)

Some people find that this is a less stressful and more enjoyable way to do email. Rather than feeling the weight of their whole to-do list, they are able to relax by engaging fully with what is immediately present. "Focusing on one thing is less stressful than panicking about fifty," says Emily, a research librarian. And Morgan, a school media specialist, comments, "Email doesn't have to be always bad. In fact, setting aside a good twenty minutes to do email and only email can be a really nice way to feel more calm and in control about those unread inbox messages."

Noticing and Dealing with Distractions

The central challenge to focusing exclusively on email is recognizing and responding to distractions. In doing the exercise, people often get a good look at their tendency to wander. "I was able to notice when my attention went off the rails," says Emily, "and was able to bring myself back to my email task. However, my attention jumped around a LOT, and I had to gently and kindly bring myself back quite often. I also had to remind myself to be kind and gentle about it, rather than frustrated."

Beyond just noticing *that* their minds wandered, people sometimes see *where* their minds went, and even *why*. "Every single time I faced an email that I didn't know immediately what to do or how I would handle it," Emily says, "I wanted to jump to a distraction, like Facebook, IM, the news, my personal email, chatting with a colleague, making tea, eating chocolate . . . anything, anything else."

Strategies for Staying Focused

Whether or not they decide to adopt this method on a regular basis, some people do come away with strategies for recovering or deepening their focus. Box 5.4 lists four commonly noted strategies.

1. Establish and monitor your intention

Establishing your intention is crucial in craftwork. It can be quite helpful to decide what you're setting out to do as you go online, and to periodically check in to see whether you are being true to that intention. Clarity of intention becomes the lodestar by which to steer your course. This is one of the most common discoveries—in all the exercises, not just this one. "I told my wife that I couldn't be interrupted for the next fifteen minutes," a management consultant named Trent says, "and I explained why (she was in the same room working, too). This seemed to elevate my focus, i.e., my stated intention actually made me more focused."

2. Use breath and body awareness to focus and relax

What can we do when we're feeling distracted? Some people discover that breath and body are powerful resources for restoring focus.

Box 5.4: Strategies for Staying Focused

1. Establish and monitor your intention
2. Use breath and body awareness to focus and relax
3. Slow down
4. Establish physical and temporal boundaries

Kathleen, a single mother returning to school, says: "In the afternoons I tend to feel fragmented, tired, and I do have a harder time concentrating. But I have started to do thirty-to-sixty-second [breath] meditations prior to opening my inbox in the afternoons and it is a huge help. Taking that short amount of time to pause the ceaseless racket in my brain before attempting to focus makes all the difference in my productivity and my emotional state."

3. Slow down

Slowing down can also help us feel more in touch and in control. It's understandable why we might check email in a rushed and breathless way: we're trying to get on to the next task, and the next (and the next . . .). But rushing is as much an attitude (I don't have time for this) as an objective fact (how much faster are we actually going, really)? Slowing down enough to take email seriously (the craft perspective again) can actually help us appreciate it, strange though this may seem. Will puts it this way: "Usually I rush through the email's contents, just scanning through the words as fast as I can, making quick judgments about its value and whether I should invest time into it. [But] when I'm committed to actually reading each email slowly, I find my experience to be a much calmer one than usual. Strangely enough, emails that I regularly would delete or find irritation with suddenly seemed kind of interesting. They seem to have value." And he adds, "I can't believe I just said email can be valuable and appreciated."

4. Establish physical and temporal boundaries

As people notice what tends to distract them, they realize that some of these conditions are actually under their control. They can eliminate potential sources of interruption, closing windows on the screen or smart phone apps, silencing their phones, clearing their desks of unnecessary clutter, and letting people around them know that they prefer not to be disturbed. Gary, an educational technologist, wrote the following guidelines for establishing such boundaries:

> Create a space conducive to focused email:
> 1. Physical: comfortable desk and chair; little noise; few outside distractions; good natural lighting
> 2. Mental: dedicate time for the exercise that puts all non-task-related thoughts outside the boundaries of practice
> 3. Social: alert others that for the next x minutes I will be focused on email and unable to converse.

Final Reflections

While this chapter's exercise is about email (or Facebook, or texting, if you prefer), the lessons from it potentially extend beyond this application to all aspects of our lives. Learning how to focus better on whatever we're doing, learning to notice those times when we're distracted and figuring out what to do about it—these are basic life skills. At the same time that we're exploring and possibly improving our email practice, we are training our attention. As Nichola comments: "I will certainly continue to explore methods of focus like this. My favorite part is the scalability: any task can be approached with the same careful attention."

Exercise 3
Observing Multitasking

I notice my attention, or lack of attention, while doing multiple tasks. In my observation notes I use the word "haphazard" a couple of times, indicating that, according to the recordings, it looks like my attention is not fully focused on what I am doing at the time. This observation tells me that I appear to get lost in what I am doing and I lose focus. Consequently, some of the most simple tasks take a while and I work very inefficiently.

—*Kathleen*

When I multitask, it's largely undirected and mindless—I'll move away from my task to check something else, with a plan to make this brief, and then end up doing other work/article reading/ Facebooking/anything for a half hour. I would like to become more mindful of these distractions—even, or especially, those simply arising in my own mind—and either ignore them or address them briefly and consciously before returning to my original task.

—*Henry*

Is multitasking a problem? Some people clearly think so. In July 2009, Clifford Nass, the late Stanford professor of communications, convened a one-day seminar on the impacts of multitasking that was attended by researchers, educators, and parents. Some of the attendees spoke to the benefits of multitasking. But a great deal of the focus, and the emotional energy, was centered on people's concerns and fears about the phenomenon. "When someone mentions multitasking, people go insane," Nass observed. Everyone involved clearly realized that more research was needed to understand the positive and negative effects of multitasking, and to provide guidance to parents and workers about when and how to do it productively and when to abstain. Rebecca Randall, of Common Sense Media, spoke to the urgency of people's concerns. "We can't wait for the longitudinal research," she said. "We need guidance now."[1]

Recent research has confirmed how common, indeed rampant, multitasking is in American culture today. For more than a decade, Gloria Mark, a professor of information science at the University of California, Irvine, has been conducting ethnographic studies of the American workplace that demonstrate the extent of the phenomenon. Her 2004 study, "'Constant, Constant, Multi-Tasking Craziness,'" surprised many people by demonstrating how often knowledge workers switch tasks. As Clive Thompson summarized these results in a 2005 article in the *New York Times Magazine,* "each employee spent only eleven minutes on any given project before being interrupted and whisked off to do something else. What's more, each eleven-minute project was itself fragmented into even shorter three-minute tasks, like answering e-mail messages, reading a Web page or working on a spreadsheet. And each time a worker was distracted from a task, it would take, on average, twenty-five minutes to return to that task."[2]

As for children, a 2010 study by the Kaiser Family Foundation, *Generation M2: Media in the Lives of 8–18-Year Olds,* reported that youth were spending more than seven hours a day "consuming media." But because they were spending so much time using more than one medium simultaneously, they were packing almost eleven hours of media content into those hours. (Although a further study hasn't yet been published, it's hard to imagine that these numbers have declined.)[3]

Research of this kind holds up a mirror to our current practices, allowing us to see what is now the case without making value judgments. But at the same time, as I indicated in Chapter 3, a growing number of studies point to the problematic side of multitasking: that it is less efficient than working on a single task and that the quality of the results may suffer. In the most dramatic case we now face, that of texting and driving, the research findings are definitive: Texting while driving is extremely dangerous.

Yet there is another side to the story. Some prominent educators and researchers argue that multitasking is a valuable, even a necessary, twenty-first-century skill. In an influential report prepared for the MacArthur Foundation, Henry Jenkins, a media scholar at the University of Southern California, has argued that today's schools ought to devote more attention to fostering new media literacy skills, among them multitasking, which he defines as "the ability to scan the environment and shift focus onto salient details." In an earlier era, he suggests, schools had primarily taught students the ability to focus narrowly on one thing, and had considered anyone who was unwilling or unable to maintain a narrow focus to be suffering from a disorder. But in today's world, he argues, both modes of attending are necessary, and neither is inherently superior to the other.[4]

The picture is further complicated by recent research suggesting that multitasking doesn't degrade *everyone's* performance. People dubbed "supertaskers," estimated to be 2.5 percent of the population, can actually perform two tasks without becoming overloaded and suffering a reduction in the quality of their output. Indeed, some of these people appear to get better when juggling two tasks.[5]

So for the most part we don't yet have the guidance that Rebecca Randall is requesting. Fortunately, I don't believe we need to wait for definitive studies to tell us how best to multitask or when to abstain. Besides, even if we had such studies, they wouldn't provide detailed guidance for each and every one of us, considering our differences in cognitive capacity, life experience, and personal preference. If we need guidance *now*, as Randall suggests, we may be able to get it by investigating our own multitasking behavior, much as we just did with email. I will show you how in this chapter, taking you through a structured exercise that parallels the email observation exercise.

Before we launch into the exercise, though, let's clarify what we're talking about. What exactly is multitasking? It basically means performing multiple activities—or "tasks"—at the same time. But there is a common misconception about what "at the same time" actually means. In most cases, we are actually attending to several activities *serially*, one at a time. Multitasking is thus rapid task switching, not maintaining simultaneous attentional contact with several objects of focus.

So multitasking essentially means moving back and forth between two or more tasks. But then whether or not you're multitasking (or you consider yourself to be multitasking) depends on what you mean by a task. When you open an email message to read the announcement of an upcoming meeting, then switch to your calendar to enter the meeting date and time, are you multitasking or simply carrying on with your current task? When you are reading an email message and notice that a new message has arrived (but you don't actually open it and read it) are you multitasking? Scholars of multitasking have offered various definitions of multitasking, but there is no general consensus about exactly what the term means.[6]

But we don't actually need an ironclad definition of multitasking for what we are aiming to accomplish here. For what we will be exploring in this chapter is how and why you shift your attention, whether you are moving between two objects in the same application (e.g., between two email messages), between two different applications (between email and Facebook), between two devices (your laptop and your cell phone), or even between online and offline activities (between texting and chatting with a friend face-to-face). How you define a task won't be as important as seeing when the shifts in your attention are effective and healthy, and when they aren't.

In investigating multitasking as an attentional practice, we will be exploring three attentional skills that are crucial to it: focusing, noticing, and choosing.

Focusing means directing your attention to the task at hand. When you are reading an email message or posting a message on someone's Facebook wall, how much attention are you paying to what you're doing?

Noticing means exercising self-observation or awareness, so you can see that other objects or activities are vying for your attention.

When your phone dings, announcing a new text message, how aware are you that this has happened? Do you consciously notice the event, or do you just respond to it out of unconscious habit?

Choosing means making a skillful, informed decision—whether to stay with your current object of focus or to switch to something else—and then reestablishing focus with whichever object you've chosen. When do you consciously choose what to attend to next (and on what basis), and when do you operate out of conditioned habit?

One last point before we dive in: I maintain an open mind about the place of multitasking in today's world. Under the right conditions, multitasking can be quite useful. And under the wrong conditions it can be counterproductive, even deadly. The challenge we face is to understand these conditions, and that's what I aim to help you do, without finger-wagging or cheerleading.

Overview of the Multitasking Observation Exercise

In the previous observation exercise, I asked you to pay careful attention to your immediate experience, to what you were thinking and feeling, while you were online. You will be doing the same in this exercise, but I will be adding some new elements that are specific to multitasking.

How to Observe Yourself

In the email observation exercise, you observed yourself the old-fashioned way, with your naked senses unaided by observational or recording technologies (other than a pencil and paper or a text editor). This may have been somewhat challenging, especially since we're not

Box 6.1: The Multitasking Observation Exercise

What to do

Engage in multitasking (task switching among several apps
and devices), using software to create a record of what you
did. Review the recordings, using the information you gather
from them to notice your habitual patterns of behavior, what
motivates them, and how these patterns affect your effectiveness and well-being.

Why do it?

• To practice (and strengthen) your ability to observe
yourself.

• To observe your current ability to focus on your
current tasks, to notice other claims on your attention,
and to choose to stay with your current task or switch to a
different one.

used to paying attention to our body, emotions, and attention while
we're online, or to checking in on our immediate experience at regular
intervals. But it is certainly doable, something we can learn and get
better at.

This kind of self-observation becomes more difficult when we're
multitasking, especially when we're in the middle of a firestorm of ac-

tivities and we're rapidly switching our focus back and forth among them. Fortunately, technology can help. There are a variety of tools that can record the activity on your desktop. Once you've obtained one of these (see Step 0 below for the details), you will be able to record yourself multitasking, and then play and replay the video to closely observe your online activity.[7]

What to Observe

As in the email observation exercise, I will ask you to make use of the mindful check-in (Appendix A) to pay attention to your experience while you're online. But in addition, I will ask you to notice your multitasking strategy: When do you decide to switch from one task to another and why? On what basis do you choose what to do next?

You may feel that you don't *have* a strategy, at least not one that you have consciously constructed. But all of us have certain habitual patterns that determine the way we multitask. Some of us respond to every interruption immediately, while others carefully limit the number of interruptions that can reach us (silencing our phones, for example) and respond selectively to the interruptions that do make it through our protective wall. By observing more closely just what you do, when, and why, you will have the chance to evaluate your current multitasking strategy and to make changes accordingly.

How to Do the Multitasking Observation Exercise

Box 6.2 summarizes the steps in the exercise.

Box 6.2: The Steps of the Multitasking Observation Exercise

Step 0: Download recording software
 Install recording software on your computer and familiarize yourself with it.

Step 1: Perform the primary practice (multitask)
 Conduct one or more multitasking sessions, using the recording software to create a video record of each session.

Step 2: Observe what you are doing and feeling
 Review the video recordings of your sessions.

Step 3: Log what you are observing
 As you replay the recordings, create a written record of what you were doing and how you felt while doing it.

Step 4: Consolidate (summarize) your observations
 Review your log, looking for larger patterns. When do you typically switch between tasks and why? When do you refrain from switching and why?

Step 5: Formulate personal guidelines
 What do these patterns suggest about how to multitask in healthier and more effective ways?

Step 6: Share and discuss
 Talk with others about what you've been discovering.

Step 0: Download recording software

Recording your multitasking sessions will simplify the task of observing yourself. Fortunately, there are a number of software tools available, some of which are free, that will do the trick. Because the technologies are changing so rapidly, I won't list any particular products or applications here. Instead, I invite you to visit my Web site, where you will find my current recommendations.[8]

If you choose a recording tool based on your own research, or select one you already have access to, you'll want a tool that at minimum allows you to record whatever is happening on your desktop, laptop, or mobile screen. In other words, when you replay your recording, you should see a movie in real time of whatever you were doing—opening and closing windows, moving them around on the screen, typing text into various windows, and so on, as well as the movement of your mouse cursor. Your tool should also let you pause the recording and restart it, and skip to other locations, just like you do when you're watching a movie, or a video clip on YouTube.

In addition, it will be helpful if your recording tool has the following capabilities:

- Saving a recording for later (re-)viewing
- Recording the sounds produced by your computer (for example, the beeps and dings that announce the arrival of new messages)
- Recording ambient sounds in your immediate environment (allowing you to hear your phone ringing or a colleague knocking on the door)

- Recording from your computer's Web cam (so you can watch your facial expressions and head movements while you are multitasking).

Before you move on to Step 1, you should not only download and install the recording software but also test it. Make a short recording (no more than a couple of minutes) to make sure the software is working properly and you know how to use it—*before* you begin to record lengthier sessions in the next step.

What if you prefer not to record your multitasking sessions in this way? Here are two alternatives. One, you can observe yourself directly, without any technical assistance, much as you did in the prior observation exercise. You may not get the wealth of detail that's available from a recording, but you should still be able to make interesting discoveries. Rather than trying to write down observations while you are multitasking (which would add one more task to your set), you might turn on an audio recorder and speak your observations out loud. Two, you can ask a friend, a colleague, or a partner, to observe you while you're multitasking and take notes. Then, at the end of the session, you can have a conversation with him or her about what happened. All the better if you are both doing the exercise, so you can take turns observing each other.

Step 1: Perform the primary practice (conduct multitasking sessions)

Now that you've figured out how to keep track of your multitasking sessions, you should conduct one or more of them, each fifteen to twenty minutes in length or longer. Which sessions should you record? I recommend that you begin with one that's fairly typical of your multitasking patterns. Find a time of day and a location when you're fairly certain to be dealing with multiple windows and applications, and perhaps also likely to be interrupted by your phone, by face-to-face contact with others, and so on. If the first session you record turns out to be unusually quiet (with little task switching), then simply try again.

Once you've got a fairly typical example, you can decide whether you want to record additional typical examples for comparison, or whether you want to explore the outer edges of your practice (or both). Let's say your normal pattern involves slow and relatively few task switches. You might choose or create a time when your multitasking will be more intense—faster and more frequent task switches than you normally engage in. Or if you're normally a pretty intense multitasker, consider creating and recording a much quieter, less dramatic session.

Finally, as you decide which sessions to record, keep the issue of personal privacy in mind. Whether you are using recording software or asking a friend to observe you, your sessions may contain information, about you or others, that is of a sensitive nature. Choose your sessions and your mode of observation carefully, so you don't violate anyone's privacy. (And if you do decide to save your recordings, whether locally or on an external server, do your best to store them securely.)

Step 2: Observe what you are doing
and feeling (watch the video)

Step 3: Log what you are observing

Once you've recorded a session, begin the observation and logging process. Watch the recording immediately, or soon after the initial session. That way, you'll be able to make use not only of what you are seeing in the recording but also your recent memories of what happened. As in the prior exercises, create a written log where, at minimum, you identify the period of the recording (many recording tools will show you the "time code" for what's currently being viewed) and take notes about what was happening at that time. (See the sample log template in Appendix B.) Pay particular attention to the following:

- As you watch the video, try to reconstruct your experience (breath, body, emotions, and attention). How did you *feel* at different points in the session, and what does this suggest to you about your multitasking practice? (If your recording includes video of your face, noticing your facial expressions and head movements may give you useful information about your emotional state. So too may the speed and direction of your cursor movements.)

- Pay special attention to the *choice points* in your session—those places where something arose that might have led you to switch to some other task. Choice points that arose because of external events will generally be easier to see. (You may be able to hear a ding on the recording when a new message arrived, or see a window change color on the screen.) But you may also be able to reconstruct choice points that arose because of events internal to you. (Perhaps the image from your Web cam shows you looking surprised, or delighted, or unhappy when you begin to read a new message, or perhaps you simply remember how you felt when that message appeared.)

- As you observe these choice points, notice how you responded to them. When did you decide to stay with your current task and when did you decide to switch? Can you reconstruct the basis for your decision?

Here are two examples of people's log entries, which they wrote while or after viewing their recordings:

Opened up four activities: (1) course homework, (2) Facebook, (3) YouTube (selected a song to play), Phone is also on, volume turned up all the way. I'm also looking at a notebook, because of my homework assignment. I need to basically reflect on the notes I took during a class. (It took me almost two whole minutes to get myself situated and set up for this assignment before I even typed anything out on my homework.)

—Nick

Facebook, paying bills, eating mindlessly. Internally knowing I am being watched with this camera so feeling initially a little on stage. Noticing how many times I touch my glasses, eat—always something in my mouth and if not food then just gum—move my feet around. Facebook still open and lots of folks responding to something I posted earlier but choosing to stick with what I am doing so that I can complete it. I also want to see more of the comments at once instead of spending time rereading and seeing who "likes" it. Impatient while a photo uploads so switch to emails. New class registrant so switch to Excel, address book, then type confirming email. Take care of that task—feels good. Noticing the heat

of the computer on my wrists and that my fingers starting to be
tense even after a week off from typing. Most of the time I look at
the keyboard when I type although sometimes trust that I know
where the keys are.

—*Christine*

Step 4: Consolidate (summarize) your observations

Having logged your multitasking sessions, you are ready to reflect on
what you've been seeing. Be on the lookout for bottlenecks and ob-
stacles, as well as places where you are operating smoothly and com-
fortably. How would you characterize your multitasking strategy? On
what basis do you shift your attention between tasks, applications, and
devices? When does this behavior seem to be productive and healthy,
and when less so? How do you keep track of your various tasks, and is
there room for improvement?

I suggest you write about the patterns you are discovering. Box 6.3
provides some questions to help you organize your thinking.

Step 5: Formulate personal guidelines

Answering these questions will most likely suggest changes you can
make. Formulate these changes as guidelines for future behavior. Some
changes may address your inner response to external circumstances
and require few or no changes in your outer activities. For example, if
you can see that when you're multitasking furiously your shoulders are
up to your ears, your breathing is shallow, and your brow is furrowed,

Box 6.3: Noticing Patterns in Your Multitasking Behavior

1. What did you do?

How many sessions did you observe? For how long? How were the sessions different from one other (e.g., did you multitask normally throughout, did you try some experiments)?

2. In observing breath, body/posture, emotions, and attention, which of these dimensions of your present experience were most salient?

What did they reveal about how you multitask?

3. In the recordings, were you able to notice when new tasks arrived and interruptions occurred (because you heard your cell phone ring or you saw a new email message appear in your inbox)?

How often did you immediately respond to the new task or interruption? On what basis?

4. In the recordings, were you able to notice the times when you did switch to another task or activity?

Why did you switch? (Note: Question 3 asks you to notice the times when you had the potential to switch. This question asks you about the times you actually did.)

5. Putting all this together, how would you characterize your current multitasking strategy?

On what basis do you decide to switch to another task, or to stay with your current task? How do you keep track of your tasks? When is this strategy most effective, and when least?

you could decide in the future to watch out for these signs of stress and to consciously relax your body.

Many changes, however, are likely to involve some alteration to your habitual mode of multitasking, to your current strategy. Have you noticed that certain internal states, such as boredom, lead you to start clicking around? Is "clicking around" a satisfying mode of operating for you? What do you want to do about it? If your mood strongly affects whether or not you are multitasking constructively, then perhaps there are times when you shouldn't engage in multitasking. And if you notice that certain forms of interruption are just too enticing to ignore but generally reduce your effectiveness, then you might consider blocking these out, to the extent you can, or working when these interruptions are less likely to arise.

As you perform this assessment, remember our earlier discussion and be mindful of unhelpful self-criticism. You may well notice behaviors you weren't previously aware of, some of which are upsetting. While a certain amount of self-judgment may be inevitable, noticing it can help prevent you from fixating on and embellishing it.

Step 6: Share and discuss

By the time we conduct this exercise in class, my students have become quite comfortable with one another and have gotten used to describing and discussing their online practices. Multitasking is such a rich phenomenon that there is a great deal to talk about as they compare and contrast their practices. I suspect you will discover this too when you share *your* discoveries. But even if you've chosen to do this exercise alone, you may just find that you can engage others in lively conversation once you tell them that you've recorded yourself multitasking.

What Others Report

Reactions to the Exercise

For some people, this is the first time they've paid conscious attention to the way they multitask. For others, it's a chance to look more closely and reflect more deeply than they've done in the past. Some of their written descriptions are quite lovely—evocative and rich in detail. Here is how Max, who works for a large tech company, describes a period of multitasking he engaged in one morning:

> I go through around a hundred new tweets in Twitteriffic, clicking on links occasionally and either reading something in the browser or adding it to my Instapaper queue to read later. I check up on Facebook and LinkedIn. I look at woot.com to see if today's deal includes a handsome, cheap TV stand, which I've been hoping to discover for months now. No luck. I read a bunch of new RSS posts in NetNewsWire, which takes me back to the browser three times. All these activities are interspersed, not discrete—I'm switching between them for no obvious reason. Coffee has that effect on me. . . . I thought I was going to be cool with sharing these videos but just watching it myself makes me uncomfortable, so I delete it.

(Max's last remark is a reference to the recording he'd made of the session. Watching it made him uncomfortable, so he decided against sharing it with other participants in the course.)

Some people can see that they like multitasking and are actually quite good at it. But even these people generally find that there's more for them to learn and improve. Others, however, don't feel nearly so good about their multitasking habits. "I am on Facebook, clicking from link to link for no reason," Sophie, a doctoral student, says. "I really felt stupid," she adds, "when I was watching myself checking Facebook three times in thirty minutes and nothing was changing, the feed was exactly the same." And Christine, a business coach, is shocked to see herself switching gears in the middle of typing a word. Even more dramatically, a graduate student named Alex has a real wakeup call when he sees himself on the video posting something on Facebook, but has no memory of having done so. "The scary part was," he says, "I watched the recording not ten minutes after doing the exercise and I couldn't remember anything about what I had written on [my cousin's] wall! Even seeing it, I didn't remember writing it."

Noticing Qualities of Body and Mind

As in the email observation exercise, people discover that their present experience—their breath, their body, their emotions, and the quality of their attention—carries valuable information about their online behavior. Kim, a part-time university instructor, comments on her breathing: "In terms of bodily feelings, I can practically see myself holding my breath. There are a few points of long sighs—a chance to exhale, finally.

Even my tendency to look to the side when I 'have to think' seems an awful lot like someone trying to find a way to breathe." By observing herself in the video, Millie, a graduate student doing health research, notices various signs of physical discomfort she was previously unaware of: holding her shoulder in a tilted, uncomfortable position and clutching her neck at times.

Some people notice that they aren't very focused while they are multitasking. "I notice my attention, or lack of attention," Kathleen says, "while doing multiple tasks. In my observation notes I use the word 'haphazard' a couple of times, indicating that . . . my attention is not fully focused on what I am doing at the time." Similarly Martin, who works at a large tech company, notices "the amount of time wasted doing essentially nothing." "I always feel like I am scrambling for time," he concludes, "yet I see where it can be easily recovered."

People also regularly take note of the strong emotions that arise while multitasking. Words like "boredom," "anxiety," "restlessness" are commonly invoked. These are discussed further in the next section, where people talk about how strong emotions motivate them to switch tasks.

To Switch or Not to Switch

The heart of the exercise is exploring when we switch tasks and why. Some switches are of course unavoidable, because a task has ended and we need to move on to something else, or because we can't make further progress on it until a new piece of information has arrived. These necessary switches aren't nearly as interesting as the optional or discretionary switches, when we're *choosing* to switch.

It is fairly easy to see how external conditions often lead us to switch tasks. When your cell phone is ringing, it can be hard to resist the temptation to answer it—or at least to notice who is calling and to make a decision based on that knowledge. It can be even harder to ignore someone talking to you in person. To varying degrees, the indicators (beeps, visual markers, etc.) that signal the arrival of a new message can also be hard to resist. Many people watching the recording of their own multitasking see the power of external interruptions to take them away from whatever they were doing at that moment.

Probably the biggest discovery people make, though, is the extent to which internal conditions—thoughts, feelings, and especially strong emotions—lead them to switch tasks, often unconsciously. They notice that task switching can be a way of avoiding what they are currently doing, a form of procrastination.

Some people also see what it was about their current tasks, or their current circumstances, that they're trying to avoid. Anxiety and boredom are often mentioned as triggers. Jonathan speaks for many people when he says, "I'll sometimes pathologically refresh inboxes and watchlists, checking to see if anything new has come in over the past thirty seconds. This is really just an indication that I'm bored. . . . It is time I could make much better use of by doing anything else in the world."

Seeing One's Overall Multitasking Strategy

By observing when they switch and why (and equally important, when they don't switch, even though they could), people are able to piece together their personal multitasking strategies—their regular habits that have emerged over years of time spent online.

Some people are *minimalist* multitaskers: they don't tend to switch tasks often, preferring to stay focused on what they're doing for long stretches of time. For them, this exercise can be exasperating, because they feel they're being asked to do something they have no inclination to do. Says Erin: "I don't think I really even understand how other people actually do multitask. . . . Maybe I am missing out on ways that I could incorporate some multitasking into my working habits. On the other hand, if it isn't broken, why fix it? . . . I've spent [many] years as a classical musician working on my focus and attention and perhaps this is just the way I am at this point."

Others are *maximalists,* tending to switch quickly and often. This may mean responding to every interruption as it occurs, in a highly reactive way. Michael, a freelance writer, decides that his standard strategy is "pretty scattershot." It involves "jumping around and looking at a bunch of different things and responding to messages, texts, and calls almost immediately when they come in."

Most of us, I suspect, are neither strict minimalists nor maximalists, but find ourselves somewhere in between. Some people notice that they have different multitasking strategies depending on a variety of conditions, including the task they are doing, their current location, or the mood they're in. "There are two ways in which I interact with multitasking," Lydia says. "One is when I am focused. This occurs when I am present mentally, and in a mood to work. In this mode, I am capable of multitasking quickly and efficiently." But when she is in the wrong mood, multitasking is a kind of flailing, "which is equivalent to

pissing in the wind—trying to do something there is no hope of suc-
ceeding with."

Others distinguish multitasking sessions in which their main aim is
to accomplish one or more tasks, to be productive, and those in which
they're simply wanting to relax, to be entertained. Will comments: "In
a session where I wasn't trying to accomplish a certain task . . . there
was less stress involved and it was more enjoyable. I could switch back
and forth from Facebook to reading an article to answering the phone
without it being a big deal. I was in no rush and I was free to impul-
sively do what I wanted and frequently did. . . . It was actually pretty relaxing and I didn't feel like I was 'multitasking' although I kind of was,
flipping from one thing to another." And in a similar vein, Max notes:
"I noticed in this exercise . . . that I do two kinds of multitasking. Sometimes I'll work my way down a to-do list getting things done and getting
distracted along the way. Sometimes I'll use the Internet as a deliberate
time sink, letting myself flit back and forth between sources of text . . .
and skimming diverse information as a means of staying informed."

Establishing Guidelines

From these kinds of observations, people are able to see the richness
and complexity of their multitasking behavior. And often, just seeing behaviors they consider counterproductive is enough to suggest
changes they might make. Since multitasking is about choice, about
deciding what to do next, many of people's guidelines address this
directly.

As in the focused email exercise, people discover the importance of
establishing their intention—what are they trying to accomplish?—as

a means of staying focused on what's most important. A technology designer named Henry writes a guideline that reads: "Work on setting out a series of tasks I want to do when I sit down at the computer. . . . Write these things down so I can keep track of what I'm working on now, whether it's in the list of set-out tasks, and whether or not I'm working on too many things at once."

This is an important first step, but what happens when the phone starts ringing, the itch to check Facebook arises, or the email begins to visibly pile up? Having seen how easy it is to respond unconsciously to such triggers, some people realize that they need to become aware of potential choice points, right at the moment they arise, and make skillful decisions about switching in the heat of the moment. Danielle, a master's student, does a lovely job of articulating both the challenge of staying focused and her proposed solution: "Often I will have a general or loose goal in my multitasking that directs my actions and switching. I feel like this works really well in most cases but sometimes does not. Where this falls apart . . . is when my attention gets 'hijacked' by a strong emotional response to something I see or read. I feel this might be solved by putting a space between that reaction and my response. Then, I can make an informed decision if I want to react to it then, later, not at all, or put off that decision." Her personal guidelines read:

> If I notice that I want to switch tasks due to a strong emotional response, take a moment to pause before switching, then reassess if I should switch or not.
>
> If I notice I am becoming impatient, try various ways to defuse that impatience before I start switching aimlessly. Take a moment to pause and reassess what my intention is.

If I notice that my attention is becoming diffuse, take a moment to focus on breathing, then reassess what my intention is and what I would like it to be. One way to do this would be to ask myself a series of questions: What am I trying to do? What would I like to do? Have I answered the question(s) I was trying to answer? Should I move on?

Final Reflections

When Eyal Ophir, Clifford Nass, and Anthony Wagner published the results of their multitasking study in 2009, they made headline news. They had recruited Stanford undergraduates, selecting fifty students who multitasked a great deal and fifty who didn't, and had given all one hundred of them a series of low-level attention tests. Their main findings were that the heavy multitaskers were worse at ignoring distractions than the light multitaskers, their memory while multitasking was worse, and they switched tasks more slowly.[9]

The sound-bite summary for these results was obvious: heavy multitaskers perform worse than light multitaskers! And it raised an important question that still hasn't been adequately answered: Do people multitask more heavily because they are unable to ignore distractions (and hence are compelled to switch tasks when they are interrupted)? Or does heavy multitasking *cause* people to become more distractible? Eyal Ophir seems to favor the second interpretation. In a 2011 interview he said: "Over time you may be training yourself NOT to focus. You teach yourself that something more exciting might be just around the corner—behind that notification, or the app on your mobile phone, or the email you haven't checked. If you prioritize the unknown, but potentially exciting, over what's in front of you, you'll have a hard time controlling your own focus. You may transition from a top-down model of attention allocation, where you decide what to focus on, to a bottom-up model, where any new notification or alert will dictate what you focus on."[10]

My guess is that both positions are likely to be true. What Ophir is suggesting sounds quite plausible. If you continually chase the latest internal or external interruption, you are missing the opportunity to strengthen your attention by bringing it back to your current task focus, "again and again." Instead, you are training yourself to pursue the latest shiny new thing that comes along, moment by moment. But it seems equally likely that if you don't have the attentional strength to avoid distractions—to notice them and bring your attention back to your original object of focus—then you will be pulled along by interruptions as they continually arise.

All this makes it sound like heavy multitasking is *necessarily* problematic. Yet in the same interview, Ophir reacts to the interviewer's suggestion that heavy multitaskers are actually less effective at multitasking. "I think heavy multitaskers are not less effective," he says, "they simply have a different goal. A different set of priorities. Where you might say traditionally we value the ability to focus through distractions, they are willing to sacrifice focus in order to make sure they don't miss an unexpected, but rewarding, surprise. As a result, they might do worse in the office scenario I described, but they might also be the first to slam on the brakes in the car/mobile phone scenario. So who is more effective?"

The central question in all of this, for me at least, is what constitutes effective behavior. When and how should we multitask, and when should we abstain? Answering this question will surely depend on understanding our current intentions or goals and matching our behavior (our strategy) to those intentions. So rather than thinking of multitasking as good or bad, we might describe it as skillful or unskillful, as effective or ineffective, as healthy or not. And doing this means looking at the behavior in its actual context—in other words, really paying attention.

Exercise 4
Focused Multitasking

I learned that there really is a way to be an efficient, mindful and productive multitasker! . . . By setting manageable intentions before I engage in multitasking, I'm able to be kind to myself while also setting a goal. This creates a place where I am better able to focus on the tasks. By taking deep breaths, I remind myself of my intention and am able to kindly refocus and bring myself back to the task.

—Kathleen

I'm still not a big fan of multitasking and I don't think that I will be engaging in a high-activity form of it with regularity. That said, the principles that I established for myself in this exercise have made the experience less frustrating. I certainly plan to adopt these strategies when I am in environments that force a degree of multitasking . . . or for times when I have a lot to accomplish and need to maintain my priorities.

—Samantha

I learned a great deal from Darlene Cohen about how to multitask in a more focused way. Darlene was a Bay Area Zen teacher, who for many years taught workshops on managing chronic illness and stress. During the dot-com boom in the late 1990s, tech workers came to her, asking her to help them work more productively and less stressfully. She began teaching workshops on "connecting with work in a deeply satisfying way," which is the subtitle of the book she eventually published on the subject, *The One Who Is Not Busy*. I discovered Darlene's work through this book, and quickly saw its relevance to my own research and teaching. In her workshops and her book she explored how we might work more effectively by training our attention and learning to shift our focus more fluidly. While reading her book, I saw the possibility of providing some experimental validation for these ideas.[1]

I contacted Darlene and explained my idea: to offer knowledge workers her training program, and to evaluate their ability to multitask both before and after the training. Darlene, it turned out, had a master's degree in neuroscience and had worked as an assistant in the Harvard laboratory of the psychologist B. F. Skinner. She was intrigued by the idea for the study and was interested in participating. With funding from the National Science Foundation and the MacArthur Foundation, and in collaboration with Jacob O. Wobbrock (a human-computer interaction researcher at the University of Washington Information School), Alfred Kaszniak (a neuropsychologist at the University of Arizona), and Marilyn Ostergren (a doctoral student at the UW Information School), I was able to recruit human resource managers from Seattle and San Francisco, train them, and test their multitasking ability.

Some of the human resource managers were trained by Darlene herself, or by one of her senior students. They received eight weeks of instruction in attention training. A second group received eight weeks of instruction in body relaxation. The third group, the waitlist control group, received no training for the initial eight-week period but was subsequently given attention training and tested again. We tested all the participants' multitasking ability, both before and after the eight-week period, putting them in an office with a laptop and a phone, and asking them to complete a series of typical office tasks, such as scheduling a meeting, finding a conference room, and writing a memo. The information they needed came via email and instant messaging, as well as documents available on paper and on their laptops. To complete the tasks in the short amount of time we gave them, they would have to multitask—answering the phone, responding to knocks on the door, and deciding when to read and answer the email and instant messages that were continually arriving. It was meant to be highly stressful, and for most participants it was.

When we analyzed the participants' tests, we found no differences across the groups in the accuracy of their results or in the amount of time they took. But other measures indicated that attention training had positively affected people's multitasking behavior. Those given eight weeks of attention training were less stressed, they had better memory for the work they had been doing, and they were less fragmented in their work, switching tasks less often and spending more time on their primary tasks. This last result is especially intriguing. Why would those given attention training have switched tasks *less often?* My guess is because they could: because with a stronger attention muscle, they could make conscious decisions about when it made sense to switch to interrupting tasks (such as a new email or instant message), and when they were better off staying with their current tasks.[2]

In addition to offering some experimental confirmation that attention training can positively affect multitasking, the study helped me formulate the two multitasking exercises I present in this book, in the previous chapter and in this one. To evaluate the study participants' multitasking abilities, we recorded their behavior and later asked human coders (undergraduates who were members of our research team) to watch the video recordings and to flag critical points in the recordings, such as when interruptions happened and when participants switched to different tasks. This led me to ask students in my course to record *themselves* and to observe *themselves,* thereby acting both as experimental subjects and as experimenting observers. In watching the recordings of the participants in our study, I was able to see, close up, the choices that people were making to shift their attention to an interruption or to stay focused on their current task. This gave me a better understanding of the attentional work that Darlene was talking about. And it helped me to formulate the exercise on focused multitasking, which is the subject of this chapter.

Overview of the Focused Multitasking Exercise

In the focused email exercise, I asked you to keep returning to your email whenever you were distracted. You might notice triggers that tempted you to go elsewhere—external triggers like your phone ringing, or internal triggers like boredom or anxiety. But in the face of these distractors, whether you simply noticed them or gave in to them (and found yourself on Facebook or Instagram), your assignment was to return to email. Again and again.

The focused multitasking exercise, of course, is different. Here the challenge isn't simply to stay focused on a single task. (If it were, you wouldn't be *multi*tasking.) The challenge in multitasking is deciding when to switch, and when not to. It is about making skillful choices. But in order to make a skillful choice, you have to realize that you *have* a choice. What makes this particularly challenging, as we saw in the last chapter, is that some of our switching behavior is habitual and unconscious. We've gone to Facebook—or to Pinterest, or YouTube, or the *New York Times,* or to our ringing phone—*before* we're even aware of the enticement these alternatives offer.

In observing their own multitasking in the previous exercise, some people begin to see the possibility of operating in a more focused and intentional way. Here Henry can clearly see not only the problem (for him), but the solution: "When I multitask, it's largely undirected and mindless. I'll move away from my task to check something else, with a plan to make this brief, and then end up doing other work. . . . I would like to become more mindful of these distractions . . . and either ignore them or address them briefly and consciously before returning to my original task." And Will notes that "multitasking seems to become unpleasant when we kind of lose control of that decision-making ability. I certainly noticed that when I was able to decide what I wanted to do and was able to act on it there was a sense of freedom and less stress."

So the focused multitasking exercise asks us to become more conscious of the attentional choices that are arising, and to make conscious decisions about how to respond to them. This means not only observing three attentional skills—focusing, noticing, and choosing—but practicing and strengthening them. When we're engaged with a task, we attempt to bring our full attention to it. When interruptions arise, we pause and notice them. And then, based on what is in our best interest, we make a choice—to switch or to stay with our current task— bringing our full attention to whatever we've chosen to focus on next.

In the focused multitasking exercise, you will have a chance to practice these skills. And I do mean *practice*. Few of us are able to consistently achieve this degree of attention. The challenge here isn't so much to "get it right" as to exercise certain skills, learning from the

---

Box 7.1: The Focused Multitasking Exercise

What to do

Engage in multitasking (task switching among several apps and devices). Focus on your current task, noticing triggers tempting you to switch, and skillfully choose whether to remain with your current task or to switch to another.

Why do it?

• To practice (and strengthen) your ability to notice when you are tempted to switch tasks (and why).

• To resist automatically/unconsciously switching tasks.

• To practice (and strengthen) your ability to choose when to switch and why.

experience, keeping in mind that the more you practice the better you will become.

How to Do the Focused Multitasking Exercise

Box 7.2 summarizes the six steps in the exercise. Let's work through each of them in turn.

Step 0: Decide how you will observe and log

In the multitasking observation exercise, I asked you to download, install, and use software to record your multitasking activity. I recommend that you do this again. But now that you've had some experience with this method, you're in a position to see how useful a second set of recordings is likely to be. So I leave it up to you to decide whether to repeat the process or, as in the earlier exercises, to log your observations on your own, either during or immediately following the exercise.

Step 1: Perform the primary practice (multitask mindfully)

Conduct one or more sessions online, choosing times of day and locations where you can expect the quality and kind of interaction and interruptions that you're wanting to investigate. Do you want to explore your multitasking ability when you're in a firestorm of activity, with phones ringing, face-to-face interruptions, your Twitter feed open, and lots of texting? Or do you prefer a quieter and slower pace of activity with a smaller number of potential interruptions?

Box 7.2: The Steps of the Focused Multitasking Exercise

Step 0: Decide how you will observe and log
Will you use the recording software from the previous exercise or not?

Step 1: Perform the primary practice (multitask mindfully)
Focus on whatever task you are currently doing, noticing triggers to switch, and skillfully choosing whether to remain with your current task or to shift to another.

Step 2: Observe what you are doing and feeling
Notice how well you are able to make conscious choices. When do you lose awareness and why?

Step 3: Log what you are observing
Create a written record of what you have been observing.

Step 4: Consolidate (summarize) your observations
Review your log, looking for larger patterns. What helps you stay focused? What typically tempts you to stray?

Step 5: Formulate personal guidelines
What do these patterns suggest about how to multitask in healthier and more effective ways?

Step 6: Share and discuss
Talk with others about what you've been discovering.

Let me suggest that you conduct at least two sessions, and that you vary the multitasking strategy in each. In one session you might try a *maximalist* strategy (where you switch often). In another you might try a *minimalist* strategy (where you try to keep your switching to a minimum). If you decide to conduct more than one multitasking session, I suggest that you try a different strategy in one of them than you normally do. In particular, if you tend to be a maximalist, try being more of minimalist and see whether you are capable of resisting the urge to switch. And if you tend toward minimalism, try stretching toward maximalism. Pushing yourself beyond your comfort zone may well teach you more about your current habits and preferences, and suggest new possibilities for your online behavior.

Step 2: Observe what you are doing and feeling

Step 3: Log what you are observing

How you handle these two steps will depend on the decision you made in Step 0 (whether or not you decided to use the recording software). If you are using the software, then you will again log your observations while you are watching the video recording of your session. And if not, you will need to log your observations either while you are multitasking or immediately afterward.

In either case, you should pay particular attention to the choices you made during the session: to switch or not to switch? When were you making conscious choices and when not? To what extent were you able to stick with your strategy (maximalist, minimalist, or somewhere in between)?

Here are two examples from student logs:

I start reading, but note right away I am cold (external trigger). I acknowledge this and oblige it because it will affect my concentration. I return, but first light a candle, then see an old one that I want to throw away. This was totally mindless action. Thankfully, I was still on task and returned to reading immediately. iTunes icon starts bouncing on desktop. It takes me roughly thirty seconds to notice it (external trigger) and I respond immediately to it. I check the voracity of the task it wants me to complete (updating credit card information) and dismiss it. If it had been shorter/easier, I probably would have responded.

—*Martin*

Simultaneous gchats make my attention shift back and forth between email and conversations. Once the chat reaches a natural pause, I'm presented with the opportunity to decide whether to return to my original task or switch to a new one. As per usual, I open many emails, click on relevant links, and once I have a series of tabs lined up, I begin to read through them.

—*Eric*

Step 4: Consolidate (summarize) your observations

Now read through your log in search of larger patterns. Were there times when it was easier to remain aware and make skillful choices? What conditions helped you to do so—changes to your breathing, to your posture, to your attitude? When did your mind tend to wander?

Which triggers, internal or external, tended to exert the most influence on you? Which ones were easy to surmount and which ones were almost impossible to resist? Did you notice any change in your response to triggers as you conducted more sessions?

Write about the patterns you have been discovering. Box 7.3 presents a series of questions that may help guide your writing.

Step 5: Formulate personal guidelines

What have you learned from this exercise that you can now put into effect? Have you discovered that a particular multitasking strategy is most satisfying for you? Are there times when you are better off not multitasking? What can you do to respond to triggers more skillfully?

Step 6: Share and discuss

This is a very challenging exercise. Aren't you curious to discover how others dealt with it?

What Others Report

Reactions to the Exercise

Yes, this is a hard exercise to do well, if this means never (or even rarely) switching tasks unconsciously. Still, some people discover benefits in multitasking in this way (more about this next), and those who set the bar low (*sometimes* being able to catch triggers and respond mindfully) seem more likely to express a degree of satisfaction.

Box 7.3: Noticing Patterns in the Focused Multitasking Exercise

1. What did you do?

How many sessions did you conduct? For how long? How were the sessions different from one other (e.g., did you multitask normally throughout, did you experiment with mimimalist or maximalist strategies)?

2. Overall, what was your experience of the exercise?

How successful were you in remaining focused? Were you able to notice choice points, pause, reflect, and make skillful choices? Were internal or external triggers easier to notice and deal with?

3. What helped you stay focused?

What conditions, either internal or external, helped you to notice triggers and to make skillful choices?

4. If you practiced more than one multitasking strategy, what did you learn from the differences between them?

5. Do you intend to adopt this method of focused multitasking in the future?

Why or why not? Would you consider at least adopting it at times?

6. Summarize what you learned from the exercise

Whether or not you intend to adopt this strategy, what did you learn that will help you multitask in the future—or help you decide when to multitask and when not to?

Some people actually change their attitude about multitasking, either about its value as a cultural practice or about their own ability to do it. "I'm still not a big fan of multitasking," says Samantha, who is completing a degree in information science, but "I plan to adopt these strategies when I am in environments that force a degree of multitasking." And Sandy, now working in the legal field, concludes that "task switching isn't always a bad thing," and "doesn't have to be a sign of procrastinating or being a stereotypical 'millennial.'"

Discovering the Benefits

What do people find helpful about this method of multitasking? I most often hear three benefits mentioned: a sense of increased productivity, reduced time, and a lessening of stress. These seem likely to be related. I noted in Chapter 3 that task switching involves "switch costs." It takes time to let go of one task and move on to another, so the more frequently we switch, the more time is spent in the process of switching and the less in attending to our tasks. This can easily affect productivity. But by being more conscious and intentional about when they switch, people may decide to switch less often. Indeed, if you can see that your desire to switch is motivated by anxiety or boredom, or that it's a form of procrastination, you may be more likely to stay with your current task.

It also seems likely that operating in a more focused, less distracted, way is less stressful. Here, for example, Stephanie makes a connection between productivity and stress: "I felt more productive and less stressed about distractions when I was mindful of them. I felt less overwhelmed, even when a distraction came up that had to be dealt with. I found it easy to return to where I was prior to the distraction."

The participants in the multitasking experiment I conducted with Darlene Cohen expressed similar sentiments. Asked how their multitasking behavior was different after their eight weeks of attention training, some of them talked about feeling calmer and in greater control. On the test after her training, one human resources manager said, "I was more calm. I was able to see things coming up and not attend to them, if they weren't urgent." Another said that on the second go-round, "I wasn't stressed. . . . I was calm about it and did one thing at a time. It was much more manageable." And a third commented: "I feel like I'm in more control, so I'm better able to manage. I'm calmer, more present, so my mind isn't going away anymore."[3]

Noticing and Dealing with Distractions

One of the explicit objectives in the multitasking observation exercise was to notice triggers or potential distractions and to observe how you typically respond to them. So it might seem that by the time people approach the focused multitasking exercise, there is nothing more to learn about distractions. But this turns out not the case. Indeed as Millie observes: "I learned a lot about my triggers in this exercise. This seemed counterintuitive to me at first, as the multitasking observation sessions seemed like the likelier place to observe my triggers. However, mindfully staying with the trigger instead of immediately [responding] to it gave me a chance to more deeply understand both the trigger source and my reaction to it."

By "mindfully staying with the trigger," people get a sense of their habitual responses to different events. Initially overwhelmed by the topic she was investigating, Emily says, "I went straight back to my inbox. . . . When I don't know what to do next, I am triggered to distract myself." "I notice I'll switch tabs when something is taking too long (i.e., more than a second, haha) to load," says Gary. And Stephanie notices how just one seemingly small move away from her current task can lead to a whole cascade of mindless clicking: "I got sucked into an email about an upcoming conference because it seemed highly relevant and was of definite interest. Sure enough, I caught myself following links and shifting into mindless clicking instead of staying focused. . . . It was almost as if allowing myself to drift for that little bit brought up thoughts of drifting more."

Of course, not all interruptions are simply to be ignored. The central challenge in the exercise is to make *skillful* choices. Says Emily: "I believe I was successful, for the most part, in deciding when to switch over to the new tasks that came in via email. I really had a sort of conversation with myself about the time it would take to switch, versus the time it would take for me to jot down a reminder to act later." And Michael observes that he did "take note of when a new email, text, or Facebook message came through, and I would recognize it and decide to check it, as opposed to the natural impulse of checking it without any prior consideration." In this way, he "recognized when something came up and made a conscious choice of whether to check it or not."

Not everyone, however, reports this degree of success. Henry describes his tendency to cascade from one diversion to another:

I was often able to notice choice points (though not always), but usually the impulse to do them was too strong to fully resist. I would like to practice at this to get a bit better at pausing before taking these actions to [decide] whether or not I really want to go, say, check email or Facebook (or Twitter or Reddit, if I'm really putting off work). Often I think the problem with this is that I convince myself that the little diversion will be a quick one— "Just go check the Facebook notifications, tick them off, and get to work," I'll say—but then I'll see an article that looks interesting, and click it . . . and then I'll read the article, and maybe it'll remind me of something else, and then I'll send an email, and then. . . . And sometime later, I'll come back to my original point of focus.

Strategies for Staying Focused

What helps us to remain focused, and to resist the various temptations and distractions that we ourselves may regard as unhelpful? I noted in Chapter 5 that people regularly describe four strategies for staying focused: establishing their intentions, returning awareness to the breath and body, slowing down, and establishing boundaries. People mention these same strategies when they've performed the focused multitasking exercise (Box 7.4).

But there is another strategy people describe after doing the focused multitasking exercise, one that isn't discussed in the earlier exercise. In focused email, the instructions are quite prescriptive and unambiguous: whenever you notice your attention wandering from email, bring it back. In the multitasking exercise, there is a great deal more latitude: *you* have to decide when to switch and when to stay with your current task. Different strategies are possible, including the minimalist and maximalist forms I mentioned above. This raises the question, which strategies are most effective for you, and when?

Box 7.4: Strategies for Staying Focused

1. Establish and monitor your intention
2. Use breath and body awareness to focus and relax
3. Slow down
4. Establish physical and temporal boundaries
5. Choose an effective multitasking strategy

Some people discover that staying toward the minimalist end (less frequent switching) helps them stay focused. "During my maximalist session," says Eric, an undergraduate studying information science, "I found that I more frequently lost my alertness and ended up checking other tabs without realizing what I was doing. . . . While engaging in my minimalist session, I was much more focused, felt more accomplished, and was able to recognize many triggers."

But some people discover that it is valuable to choose a strategy based on their current circumstances. Thus Morgan observes:

Being honest with myself up front about what needs to get done (or doesn't) at a particular work session is really important. Once I've decided if it's okay to multitask or that I need to focus mostly on one task at a time to completion, I quickly settle into that mode of working, and distractions are dealt with much more easily. In the former situation, I'm extremely focused, and no amount of inbox numbers running up can distract me until I'm done with the task at hand. In the latter, I still get things done but don't feel bad about the occasional Pinterest jaunt or email switchover in between the actual work. It's nice to know that I'm capable of both of these styles and I think they'll be really helpful in the future.

Final Reflections

When I first conceived of the multitasking experiment, I described it to a friend, who counseled me not to undertake it. She was concerned that training people to be better multitaskers—at the extreme, training people to become more efficient, machinelike workers—might just feed today's mania for going ever faster and producing ever more, health and well-being be damned. Shouldn't we multitask less, she was suggesting, not better? (Indeed, after the study was published and received press attention, some people expressed criticism of exactly this kind.)

To be honest, I had some of these same concerns—and my friend knew it. But I felt then, and feel even more strongly now, that the training in focused multitasking is meant to increase our options, to increase our freedom to choose what is skillful and healthy. As we saw in Chapter 5, some people find freedom in focusing exclusively on a single task or app. Emily, for example, said that focusing on one thing was less stressful than panicking about fifty. She thus came to see that *not* multitasking was a real option, and that it worked for her.

But I doubt that Emily was suggesting she would never multitask again. There are times when many of us will find ourselves multitasking, either because we have unconsciously entered into it or because we chose to do so. And the focused multitasking exercise suggests that it is possible to multitask in a calmer and more focused way. Discovering that we can shift our focus with greater awareness and skill thus gives us more options. We have the freedom to choose to multitask, or not, depending on the circumstances. I see from student responses that they generally understand this (as the quotation above from Morgan makes clear).

What's more, whether or not we choose to practice focused multitasking, the skills involved are general life skills—they will help us to craft a better life. For we are continually shifting our attention from one object of focus to another. And the character and quality of our lives is in large measure determined by the choices we are constantly making about what to attend to next and what to do about it. Learning to observe this behavior, to make it more conscious, and to make skillful choices can therefore help us stay focused when it really matters, and to shift our attention when it is appropriate. The lesson is simple conceptually, even as it takes much practice to learn. As Erin puts it in one of her personal guidelines: "Be mindful and make your decisions—don't let your decisions make you."

Exercise 5
Mindful Unplugging

I noticed my breath, body, and emotions most when I was outside walking to and from class. Because I wasn't feeling anxious about when I would receive the next text or notification, I noticed myself taking deeper and steadier breaths. At times, I felt very content because I was observing my surroundings. This happiness peaked during the day, when I was walking around outside.

—Nina

Having established that I wasn't allowed to check Facebook took off any pressure I might otherwise feel to check it, and made me realize how much pressure I do sometimes feel to check the site.... Telling myself I simply wasn't allowed to check the site freed me of this. I was able to acknowledge that, realize I probably wasn't really missing anything important, and do something else.

—Henry

When I notice the internal tug to engage with email or Facebook and there is not a real need, I will be mindful of it and ask my-

self "Why?" I might still engage with these technologies, even
if a "need" does not exist, but it will be with a more mindful
interaction.

—Kathleen

In the preceding chapters, we've explored a single information
practice, such as email, as well as the interleaving of multiple practices. You've seen how it's possible to carefully observe your current online habits, noticing what's working well and what isn't, and to
use these observations as the basis for making helpful changes. You've
also seen how it's possible to adopt a more focused attitude toward
a single practice—or even toward multitasking—so that you're better
able to focus on the task at hand and bring yourself back to it when
your attention wanders. The emphasis of all this work has been on
your online activity.

But none of us is online, or plugged in, all the time—although
some of us may be approaching such a state of affairs. There are times
in the day when we're not using a laptop or a cell phone, when we're
not listening to music through earphones, when we're not watching
TV or listening to the radio. This may be because we're unintention-
ally separated from our devices (we accidentally left our phone home),
because we've lost Internet or cell phone access, because we're forbidden access in certain social settings, because we've consciously chosen
to unplug, or because we're asleep and unconscious.

In recent years a cultural discussion has opened up around the
meaning and value of being unplugged. Some of this discussion has focused on the importance of being completely offline—going completely
device-free—while some of it has focused more on limiting access to

certain media and technologies, such as video games, or restricting access in certain social settings or for certain age groups. Questions being asked today include: Should infants be forbidden screen time before a certain age? How much television or video gaming is acceptable for children at different ages? Which, if any, digital technologies should be permitted in the classroom? How much value is there in creating "tech Sabbaths" or regular "Sabbath time"—periods when individuals, families, and groups agree to disengage from the swirl of digital media and technologies?

In addition to discussing and debating the merits and methods of unplugging, more and more people have actually been *experimenting* with unplugging. These experiments are taking place in schools, in workplaces, and in families. There is even a national movement, which has organized an annual National Day of Unplugging. Drawing their inspiration from the traditional notion of the Sabbath, the founders of this initiative have created a "Sabbath Manifesto."[1]

As first articulated in Judaism, and later taken up by Christianity and Islam, the Sabbath is a day of rest, a day to disengage from mainstream market culture. While in its origins it is clearly a religious institution, it has left a major impression on secular culture, giving rise to the modern notion of the weekend. In the 1820s in the United States, the Christian Sabbatarian movement used its belief in the sanctity of the Sabbath to make Sunday a nonwork day. And in the 1920s, American Jewish and labor leaders were successful in claiming Saturday as a second "day off." Time will tell whether this secular formulation of Sabbath time, centered on our devices, will catch on, and whether it can counteract the breakdown of the distinction between the workweek and weekend, which took a hundred years of political activism to establish.[2]

If you take the Sabbath as a literal model for unplugging—as the organizers of the National Day of Unplugging have done—then for a twenty-four-hour period you would abstain from *all* digital media and technology. This may work for some of us. But it is hardly the only possibility. Deciding which technologies to abstain from and when is a complex process, one that we will investigate in this chapter.

Ultimately, I believe, unplugging can help us discover an appropriate balance between our online and our offline activities. When is being online worthwhile and healthy: when does it truly serve our purposes? And when is it unhelpful or unhealthy: when does it distract us from what matters most? I don't believe that there is just one right answer to these questions, for all people, for all times. The answers we arrive at will depend on a variety of factors, including our cognitive and emotional makeup, our stage in life, our current life circumstances. There is just no substitute for investigating these circumstances for ourselves. And this is what I will help you do as you decide what to unplug from and for how long, and as you formulate personal guidelines for your future online and offline behavior.

When we disengage from the devices and apps we use regularly, it should hardly be surprising if we miss them, even long for them at times. To characterize this relationship, we sometimes say we are "addicted." Indeed, at various points in the exercises, my students will use this word, as Sophie does when she says, with a touch of humor: "I am an email addict and if there was an institution or a rehab center for email addicts, I would definitely join." References to addiction appear most frequently in the unplugging exercise, perhaps because it is here that students are asked to abstain from significant technologies and apps for a day or more. Yet there is potentially a difference between our common, everyday use of the word and its clinical meaning. And, it turns out, there is currently a debate within the scientific community about what it means to be addicted to a digital technology or an app— and even whether the term "addiction" is appropriate. If this is of interest or concern to you, I refer you to Appendix E, where I summarize the current debate and offer you my own view on the matter.

Overview of the Mindful Unplugging Exercise

At heart this exercise is quite simple: *Stop* engaging in certain online practices for a period of time and *observe* what happens. To do this, you will need to make two main decisions: which practices and technologies to abstain from and for what period of time. Let's consider each of these decisions in turn.

First, what should you give up? It would be ideal if you could abstain from *all* digital information technologies and practices for a period of time. Of course, to do so, you'd have to decide for yourself what "all" actually means—a word that in this case is clearly open to interpretation. You might decide, as some people do, not to use any of your main digital devices (your laptop, phone, or tablet) and any of the applications that run on them. But if your life circumstances make it difficult to do this, you might add back certain practices or apps that you just can't do without during the period of the fast—making phone calls, for example. Or, taking a minimalist approach, you could decide just to give up one practice or application, such as email or Facebook. Whatever you choose to abstain from, though, make sure that it has a real and important place in your life. Obviously, there's little point in letting go of something that's unimportant or rarely used.

Second, how long should your fast last? Here too, the decision is yours. I suggest a minimum of twenty-four hours—long enough to go through a whole cycle of your life during which the absence of the technologies and practices will matter. But what if you are unable to maintain the fast for the period of time you've blocked out? So be it. The difficulty in sticking to your plan becomes part of the exercise, and something you can reflect upon and learn from.

So much for *stopping*. What about *observing?* If you've been doing the exercises in the book (or have at least read the earlier exercise chapters), you know that I have emphasized the importance of observing your immediate experience: whatever is going on in your mind and body. Noticing how you react to abstaining will shed light on how the absent technologies or practices normally affect you. (You may want to review the mindful check-in, introduced in Chapter 3 and more fully explained in Appendix A, as a technique for noting your immediate experience.) In addition, it will be important to pay attention to the triggers that arise—internal and external events that prompt you to engage with the technologies and practices that are now off-limits.

How to Do the Mindful Unplugging Exercise

Box 8.2 summarizes the steps in the exercise.

Step 1: Perform the primary practice (unplug)

You will need to make two main decisions before you begin: (a) which media, technologies, and practices to abstain from; and (b) over what period of time to do so. Be sure to choose technologies or practices that

Box 8.1: The Mindful Unplugging Exercise

What to do

Abstain from using one or more apps or devices for a twenty-four-hour period or longer. Observe the effects of the fast on your mind and body.

Why do it?

  • To notice when, how, and why certain apps and devices exert an unhelpful pull upon you.

  • To investigate how to achieve a better balance between your online and your offline activities.

matter to you—whose absence you will miss. Also be sure to choose a substantial enough period of time, one that is long enough to be noteworthy, and during a time period when you would normally use the technologies you're abstaining from.

Step 2: Observe what you are doing and feeling

In this exercise you are interrupting your normal patterns of use. So there are likely to be times when you would ordinarily reach for your cell phone, or check email or Facebook. Notice the impulse to do so. What is going on in your mind and body, or in the external world, that has triggered the desire to go online? Or if you suddenly find yourself

Box 8.2: The Steps of the Mindful Unplugging Exercise

Step 1: Perform the primary practice (unplug)
For the period you've decided upon, abstain from the media and technologies you've selected.

Step 2: Observe what you are doing and feeling
Pay attention to the impulses and feelings that arise in response to being unplugged.

Step 3: Log what you are observing
Keep a running record of what you observe during the period of the fast.

Step 4: Consolidate (summarize) your observations
Review your log, looking for larger patterns. What is the effect on you of being unplugged? What does this tell you about your relationship to the media and technologies you're abstaining from?

Step 5: Formulate personal guidelines
What do these patterns suggest about how to use the technologies in question in healthier and more effective ways? In the future, when would it be good to unplug?

Step 6: Share and discuss
Talk with others about what you've been discovering.

online, in violation of the fast, notice how *that* feels, and see whether you can reconstruct how you got there. Notice too whether there are stretches when you might have been tempted to access the application or device but didn't (and perhaps felt no impulse do so). How does *that* feel?

Step 3: Log what you are observing

As in the previous exercises, you will want to maintain some kind of written record. In the earlier cases, however, you were typically performing the exercise for a relatively short period of time—for twenty minutes, a half-hour, or an hour. But in this exercise, the period of exploration will probably extend for one or more days. It probably doesn't make sense to take notes constantly, so you'll have to figure out a practice of note taking that is useful—that provides you with enough relevant detail—but doesn't overwhelm you.

Here is the transcript of an instant-messaging conversation Emily logged during the three days she abstained from Facebook:

> 10:22 AM
> Me: i miss facebook
> Friend: AHAHAHAHAHAHAHAH
> you are in love with facebook
> Me: i just broke up with facebook
> my heart is broken
> 10:34 AM
> Me: oh shit.
> i just went blindly to facebook

slammed it shut before i read anything
i only lasted one hour.
Friend: AHAHAHAHAHAHAHAH

On the completion of her fast, Emily noted: "Sunday morning rolled around, and I was allowed to go back to Facebook. I did so, greedily, and was disappointed. It wasn't fulfilling. I wasn't really missing anything when I was gone."

Step 4: Consolidate (summarize) your observations

Once you've logged your experience of the fast, you should step back to see what this is telling you about your relationship with the practices and technologies you've abstained from. Do you feel that you currently have the balance right, or do you need to adjust the amount and timing of your use of the technologies in question? Box 8.3 offers some questions that may help guide your reflection.

Step 5: Formulate personal guidelines

Now encode your discoveries as personal guidelines.

Step 6: Share and discuss

As you'll see in the next section, there is a great deal of variation in what people discover in the process of unplugging. You may be surprised by how differently your friends, colleagues, or family members approach this exercise when you share your discoveries with them.

Box 8.3: Noticing Patterns in Your Unplugging

1. What did you do?

What did you choose to abstain from and why? (What is your normal practice with these technologies?) For what period of time did you decide to abstain?

2. Overall, what was your experience of the exercise?

How successful were you in maintaining the fast? What helped or hurt you in maintaining it?

3. How successful were you in noticing the impulse to go online?

Were you generally able to notice triggers before you reacted to them? Why or why not?

4. How did the fast affect your mind and body?

What did you notice about your breath, your body, your emotions, and your attention during the period of the fast? Did your reactions vary depending on time of day, internal or external factors?

5. Did your response to the fast change over time?

Did it get easier the longer you maintained it, or perhaps harder?

6. Summarize what you learned from the exercise

What does this exercise tell you about your relationship with these technologies/practices—about how and when to use them effectively, and about when to unplug?

What Others Report

Reactions to the Exercise

This exercise gives people a great deal of latitude in what they abstain from and for how long, and the choices people make are quite diverse. The main pattern I have observed is that people often choose to disengage from social media—from Facebook, in particular. I take this as an indication of our mixed feelings about social media, and the questions we are now wrestling with about face-to-face versus online relationships.

Most people are quite successful at maintaining the fast and feel good about it. "Overall, I would say my experience was positive. By this I mean that I was successful in not checking email or Facebook for a little more than two days," says Kathleen. "All in all, it was one of the best days I had had in a long time. I only wish that I could have shut down the computer altogether," says Heather. "I welcomed the silence and the relief of pressure," says Melissa, a school administrator. And Eric is surprised to discover how easy it was: "When I started my fast, I was a little anxious about not having access to my phone. . . . I thought I was going to be fidgety and bored all day, but this wasn't the case at all."

Inevitably, of course, other people report more mixed reactions. Some report lapses. Having chosen to abstain from Facebook, Danielle says, "I started reading the Facebook comments without thinking and read through one before I remembered." (Here she echoes what Emily said in the log entry I quoted above.) And some report finding the exercise quite hard. Says Martin: "I found the experience . . . strange. The pull to go to my computer was huge anytime I felt a little bored or just unsure of what to do next with my day. The same goes for the phone. I did have the device in my pocket, but I was shocked how often I found myself pulling it out with the intention to check the Internet or email." For some, at least, abstaining becomes easier over time. "After the first day," Samantha says, "it was a lot easier for me to stay focused on my present activities and mindful breathing was really helpful for diverting my attention when I felt the impulse to stray."

Discovering the Benefits of Unplugging

Here, as in the focused multitasking exercise, the three main benefits people describe have to do with increased productivity and focus, better use of their time, and greater relaxation (reduction in stress). This makes sense, since both of these exercises give people a chance to notice and reduce their reliance on inessential and distracting uses of the technologies.

Regarding productivity, an undergraduate named Nina pursuing a degree in media studies observed, "I was able to focus a little better on my tasks. Instead of taking breaks to check my phone every couple of minutes, I was able to stick to a task without becoming as distracted." (Nina had given up the use of her phone for twenty-four hours.) And Heather exclaimed, "It was a miracle!! By making a deal with myself that I would not get sucked into timewasting activities, I actually got that [work] done, and pretty well, I think, in about four hours. I was flabbergasted." (She had unplugged for twenty-four hours from Facebook, a blog on NPR, the Huffington Post app on her phone, and texting.)

Then too, various people commented that unplugging gave them more time to spend on other important activities, such as (offline) reading, walking the dog, and "talking to my grandma on the phone." Most dramatic (and touching), some people reported reorienting to nature. Thus Nina says: "After I got to work, I was waiting for the crosswalk to turn white, and reached into my pocket to find my phone again. I realized that my phone usually fills those small spaces in the day during which I am waiting to do something else. Because I couldn't play with my phone while waiting for the crosswalk, I looked up at the sky, which I realized I rarely do. This felt good. Normally I am so engaged with my phone that I don't even process my surroundings. Sometimes this even causes me to feel nauseous. It was refreshing to take in the city and smell the fresh air."

And Krista reported seeing, while walking to the gym, "several plants sprouting the first new colors." She was tempted to take a photo with her phone, but resisted. "Would I have noticed the color as fully as I did if I had sent that picture? Possibly, but the very act of resistance helped me recognize that the first sign of spring—in and of itself—is valuable to me as an individual, and not just because it serves as a point of conversation between me and someone else."

Finally, some described feeling more relaxed. "After a while," Nina says, "I forgot that I didn't have my phone with me. I found that I was more relaxed, had steadier breathing and was more able to focus." Henry noticed that "a feeling of relief would come over me" when he realized he couldn't check social media. And Eric found that he had such a relaxing day unplugged that he felt anxious about ending his fast.

Noticing the Pull of Absent Media

Because they have abstained from certain tools and devices, people are able to experience the lure of these now forbidden things. As Martin puts it, "Nothing can let you know how strong the pull [of technology] is until it isn't there anymore." And feeling this pull sometimes leads them to further investigate: Why is Facebook, or email, or surfing the Web so important to me at this very moment, even after I've decided to abstain from it?

Martin decides that it is a form of escape: "I was struck by the frequency of feeling a pull towards getting onto my computer or accessing the Internet. It really made me question how much time I waste on that stuff—time that could be better spent. It also made me reflect on the escapism that it presents. Escape from my current state of mind, from doing a difficult task, from anything." Dana, a young master's student, also uses the word "escape," reporting that she watches a great deal of TV as "a form of escape for me to avoid feeling overwhelmed by the information I am learning, as well as to avoid feeling lonely."

Kathleen concludes that the urge to check email or Facebook often comes when "I am bored, curious or looking for some kind of interaction with community." Emily reports that "I went to Facebook when I didn't know what to do next, or whenever I was transitioning to a new task." Diane notices that without access to Facebook she feels the anxiety of missing out: "I felt jittery, worried that someone would communicate something important and I would miss it, or they would think I was avoiding them." Erin echoes this when she notes she was anxious "throughout the email-free day, when I was worried that there might be something I was missing, or when I felt guilty for not communicating my whereabouts."

Lydia concludes that she constantly checks social media when she is forced to wait for something: "Why the incessant need to check? Because I did not want to be in that moment of waiting for the bus to arrive, waiting for the bus to deliver me, waiting for Guffman, waiting for the coffee to be made, waiting for class to start. Waiting. I did not want to be waiting for anything. I wanted to be active with my school work. Complete work tasks. Remove myself from the head spin of stressing over my to-do list, not waiting. It's clear to me that I have been using this outlet as a way to disassociate from the moment because I am overwhelmed."

And last, Henry notices not only what draws him to social media but what he calls its "addicting circle"—how use seems to encourage more use: "I'm becoming more aware of social media . . . as a kind of 'circular' system. . . . That is to say, . . . the more I interact with Facebook (posting, messaging, liking or commenting on posts, etc.), the more the site will, in a way, 'demand of' and notify me—I'll get more notifications, more additional comments to read, more likes, more messages, and on and on. This, of course, is a (potentially addicting) circle—these things feel good, but also consume lots of time. I've found that the less I use Facebook, the less rewarding it is when I do use it (anytime I log on, I have fewer comments to read, fewer notifications, etc.)—and while this can be mildly disappointing when I do check the site, it also greatly lowers the temptation to log on."

Discovering Strategies That Help Maintain the Fast

What helps people resist the lure of the technologies they are abstaining from? In Box 8.4, I list three strategies that people regularly mention.

Box 8.4: Strategies for Resisting the Pull

1. Hiding devices, closing apps, etc.
2. Noticing triggers and pausing
3. Engaging in other activities

1. Hiding devices, closing apps, etc.

"Out of sight, out of mind." While putting devices away, turning off ringers, and closing apps isn't a foolproof strategy for eliminating the lure of our digital tools, it can certainly help. Thus Nina decides to keep her phone in her backpack rather than in her hand or pocket. Sophie switches it to silent mode. Martin talks about "leaving devices at home . . . or removing them from my periphery."

2. Noticing triggers and pausing

One of the most useful skills involves noticing triggering events that may lure us back to the tools and apps we're abstaining from. If we can notice the trigger before reacting, we have the potential to pause long enough to address it. Some people find that bringing their attention back to their breathing can help with this. Nichola noticed that when she goes for a walk, "I get a bit antsy in public places if I don't have my phone to distract me, so I tried to just pay attention to my breathing and it helped." Others find it is helpful to recall their current intention and priorities. Kathleen says, "Awareness of the intention I set to not engage in these technologies . . . helped, especially in moments when I would normally engage."

3. Engaging in other activities

A third strategy some report is occupying themselves with fulfilling offline activities—the kinds of activities that excessive time online had previously prevented them from enjoying. What helped Kathleen maintain her fast was "doing things: a hike, a run, an evening out. . . . I just generally stayed busy."

Searching for Balance

The point of this exercise is to discover a constructive balance between your online and your offline activities. To be sure, a dimension of the investigation is discovering what's *not* constructive, as we've seen in the observations people make above. But I have no hidden agenda here— I'm not trying to get people off Facebook, to stop them from multitasking. The participants in my classes and workshops clearly understand this, and they write and speak regularly about their own search for balance, reaching beyond simplistic ideas of good or bad, right or wrong.

Heather, for example, now sees how complex is her relationship with the technologies: "I have found that my relationships with these technologies are more complex than I had assumed, but I am not judging them to be negative, just 'more complex.' Through this exercise I became more aware of my choices and habits and I remembered that I have control over both of these things!"

Emily arrives at a new understanding of the place of Facebook in her life, one in which it still matters but will play a less dominant role:

> I would like to be more creative and less passive. These digital information technologies are a passive outlet for distraction, and

inhabit a separate online life, and I need to find a balance to feel
like a whole person. I blindly and immediately head to Facebook because it's a quick and easy window into other people's
lives. It's juicy, but also mundane. It has its place, and I'll keep
it in my life, for now, but I do want to remember that feeling of
going back to Facebook after three days. It was a letdown. I'd
like to live my own life more fully. . . . I'll continue to use it . . .
but will try to keep that in mind and use it as a place to share
and connect, rather than brag about my own life or judge
others'.

And Erin reports on her discovery that Facebook and email play
very different roles in her life, and need to be treated differently:

When I finally returned to Facebook, I was disappointed. Sure,
there were plenty of new posts to read, but nothing worth the
twinges of curiosity that abstaining from it had caused. Email,
however, was a different story. Perhaps because I do more daily
tasks and communication over email than Facebook, I had a lot
more to catch up on when I returned to it. Yes, of course there
were plenty of messages that I could just ignore, like always, but
there was a more concentrated session of email to deal with the
results of my fast. As opposed to Facebook, when I got back to
email I was relieved—both that I hadn't missed anything truly
disastrous or significant (though there was stuff to catch up on
for work, especially) but also I was relieved to be back in contact.
I've had a similar feeling when returning from a long camping trip
outside of cell phone range.

With these newfound insights, people write a wide range of personal guidelines. Some people do say that they want to build a regular, Sabbath-time fast into their lives. Says Danielle, "I like the realization of control I have over the tech in my life and how personalized I can make every Sabbath, if I want. I realize that I like the fast, I find it contributes to my well-being, and I would like to explore how I can incorporate this into my life on a more regular basis." Morgan decides that she'd like to adopt a partial Sabbath on weekends, where "I try not to be on social networking sites and email much at all over weekends where I have the ability to disengage." "I hope that by modeling things like this," she adds, "it'll also rub off on my husband. =)."

Others realize that smaller breaks will serve them better. Susan, who has worked as an executive assistant, says that she "would like to take more breaks from technology or breaks from being so available" on social media. Megan, a master's student in her mid-twenties, decides that she will "make an effort to incorporate nondigital activities into my brain breaks; leaving the computer for a few minutes might be a more effective way of maintaining my productivity when I return to my task than simply spending time using my computer in a different way." And Amy, a primary school teacher, writes this guideline: "Take consciousness breaks. Breathing, listening, feeling my body on the chair. Pay attention to my body and listen to my inner voice."

Some people decide that they will continue to work on noticing and responding to their triggers. Says Samantha: "Going forward, I would like to be more mindful in my use of social media. Before jumping into these activities, I want to be able to pause and ask myself if I'm doing it because I want to or because I feel like I *need* to. I think making this distinction will help me engage in positive, enjoyable ways that don't interfere with other areas of my life." On a similar note Kathleen says: "When I notice the internal tug to engage with email or Facebook and there is not a real need, I will be mindful of it and ask myself 'Why?' I might still engage with these technologies, even if a 'need' does not exist, but it will be with a more mindful interaction."

Being more mindful and asking "Why?" This nicely summarizes the point of the unplugging exercise. Abstaining disrupts the habits we've developed around our digital tools. It helps create a space between the trigger and the automatic reaction, a pause, and in that moment of greater awareness we can ask, "Why am I doing this?" From this question helpful insights can arise.

Final Reflections

Clearly, unplugging works. When people take it seriously, when they make a real commitment to abstaining from certain online activities, they discover how to achieve greater balance in their lives. But what does balance really mean here? As we've seen, it generally means fine-tuning how and when we're online, and for nearly everyone I've encountered, this means *reducing* the amount of time they are engaging with their digital tools. These tools exert a powerful pull, and when we look more closely at how we're spending our time, we realize that some of our time online is counterproductive, wasteful, and unfulfilling. The trick is sorting the wheat from the chaff, so that we can see which behaviors are helpful and fulfilling and which aren't, and can then make conscious decisions about how to proceed.

Unplugging may seem like an individual decision—each one of us figuring out how to achieve the balance that is uniquely right for us.

Indeed, to a large extent it is. But we will miss an important part of the challenge if we think that achieving balance is *only* a matter of personal or individual choice. For there are powerful cultural forces at work that aim to keep us plugged in. We live in a "more-faster-better" culture where "more is not enough" (to quote the subtitle of a 2005 book called *American Mania*). Clearly, there is a powerful cultural imperative to do more, to produce more, and to do so ever more efficiently. And to the extent that we have internalized this imperative (which I believe many of us have, including me), it can be hard to take a break, to step away from the machine—especially when we feel the subtle pressure of our ever-present to-do lists.[3]

What's more, our digital devices aren't only our work machines, but also the places where we shop, entertain ourselves, and communicate with loved ones. Taking a break from work can therefore mean switching to other apps or Web sites on the same device, rather than going for a walk or reading a book. While watching a YouTube video or communicating with friends on Facebook isn't productive for our work, it can still be highly productive in economic terms. Companies like Google and Facebook have earned huge profits through advertising, and the longer we stay online, clicking around, the more likely we are to buy, and the more personal data these companies can collect about us. (A recent book, *Hooked: How to Build Habit-Forming Products*, presents and celebrates this strategy.)[4]

In other words, the pressure to stay online arises not only from our individual propensities but from the cultural conditioning to produce and consume ever more. It is not unlike the challenge we face to eat healthfully. Today's obesity epidemic is in part the result of choices the food industry has made—to market drinks with high sugar content and food with high fat content, for example. As individuals, we can choose to eat healthful amounts and kinds of food, and we should. But we also can and should work at the societal level to shift the patterns of food production and consumption. What would it look like if the technology industry aimed to promote balance, rather than seemingly endless consumption? And what forms of social and political action might help bring this about?

Honing Our Digital Craft

By the time they have completed these five exercises, my students have learned quite a lot. They have explored their habitual ways of operating online, noticed when these largely unconscious patterns have worked well for them and when they haven't, and prepared guidelines that reflect their new understandings of how to conduct themselves online in the future. As a final assignment, I ask them to write one last reflection that summarizes what they've learned from the exercises and from the ten-week-long conversation with their fellow students and with me. Now that you and I have arrived at this point, I want to offer you *my* reflections—my summary of this process and the kinds of insights it leads to—based not just on what I've observed in my students but also what I've noticed about my own digital craftwork.

The Stages of Digital Craft

At the beginning of the book, I suggested that we might profitably view our digital activities as a kind of craftwork. Doing this, I suggested, would help us to see how to improve the quality of our online activities by noticing certain parallels with sports and handcrafts. We could enhance our performance by adopting a certain attitude: being intentional or purposeful about what we were setting out to accomplish and by caring enough to do it well. And this caring could be realized by bringing the best of our embodied skills to bear and by engaging in an ongoing process of learning.

Now I want to introduce one additional dimension of craftwork, which I will use to further organize the kinds of learning that emerge from the exercises: Craftwork proceeds in stages. The central stage, of course, is the actual doing, the performance. This is when the calligrapher deposits ink on the page, when the cellist plays her instrument, when the tennis player engages in the game. But there are actually two other stages, which are no less necessary because they are less visible: preparing and finishing. Indeed, there would be no well-tuned performances without these two other stages. In the preparatory stage, the calligrapher makes sure his tools are sharp and ready to hand, the cellist tunes her instrument, and the tennis player stretches and prepares himself mentally for the match. And once the performance is over, the craftsperson tends to her body and her tools, in preparation for moving on to something else.

Tim Ingold, an anthropologist at the University of Aberdeen who has extensively studied handcrafts, illustrates these three stages by describing the process of cutting a plank of wood with a saw. First is the preparation: collecting the tools and materials, sharpening the saw, measuring and marking the plank, and making the initial cut. Then comes the main performance: the rhythmical sawing of the board. And finally the finishing up: the delicate last cuts to sever the two pieces of board, and the cleanup or preparation for the next woodworking activity.[1]

Ingold draws an analogy between doing craftwork and taking a journey. Think, for example, about the work involved in taking a family vacation. The preparatory phase includes the planning (where shall we go? how long shall we stay?), the packing, and locking up the house. Then comes the travel itself: the hours in the car, the decisions about where to eat and how to respond to local driving conditions. Last is the arrival at the destination and the various rituals associated with that: checking in, unpacking, and settling in.

Once pointed out, these stages seem pretty obvious. Everything, in a sense, has a beginning, a middle, and an end. But what I've noticed over years of helping people observe their online behavior is that we rarely pay much attention to the requirements of these different stages. As you have probably seen in the exercises, we often drift online without much clarity of intention. We wander through one or more tasks without the focus the work deserves. And we miss the opportunity to pause or rest when we're done. But in performing the exercises in this book, people discover a number of ways to counter these tendencies.

In Box 9.1 I have tried to summarize the main discoveries people make by organizing them according to the stages to which they apply. But just to be clear: I don't mean to suggest that everyone does (or should) make all these discoveries. As I've said throughout the book, no one set of rules or guidelines will apply to all of us across differences in age, culture, context, cognitive and emotional predisposition, and so on. Still, I think there is something quite useful in reflecting on what we've been learning by noticing the stage of craftwork where they most readily apply.

Box 9.1: The Stages of Our Digital Craftwork

Stage 1: Preparing

- Clarify your intention: What are you aiming to accomplish?
- Establish focus: Can you bring sufficient focus to your current task? What do you need to do to deepen your focus?
- Prepare your body: Can you adopt a relaxed and attentive posture? What stands in the way?
- Prepare your environment: Is your environment free of unnecessary distractions?

Stage 2: Performing

- Steer a successful course by noticing choice points and choosing how to respond to them in order to stay true to your intention.
- As you proceed, periodically return to the points in Stage 1. Are you still true to your intention? Is your degree of focus sufficient for what you're doing? Is your body (still) in a state of relaxed readiness? Is your environment (still) conducive to what you're doing?

Stage 3: Finishing

- Notice natural break points, when you can pause or stop. (Notice the temptation not to pause or stop.)
- In pausing or stopping, let go of what you were just doing. Is switching to another online activity helpful, or is it a way to avoid pausing and resting?
- Clean up: Put your tools away, closing windows and apps, putting physical materials away.

In the remainder of this chapter, as a further means of summarizing what we've explored, I will discuss some of the themes that are central to this work. Let's begin with what for me may be the most important of these themes: the importance of choice.

The Importance (and the Place) of Choice

In his 2004 book *The Paradox of Choice: Why More Is Less,* Barry Schwartz, a social psychologist at Swarthmore College, pointed to the problem of living in a culture with an overwhelming abundance of choice. "When people have no choice, life is almost unbearable," he observed. But "as the number of available choices increases, as it has in our consumer culture, the autonomy, control, and liberation this variety brings are powerful and positive. But as the number of choices keeps growing, negative aspects of having a multitude of options begin to appear. As the number of choices grows further, the negatives escalate until we become overloaded. At this point, choice no longer liberates, but debilitates." The challenge for us is to determine when choice liberates and when it debilitates.[2]

Our online choices are sometimes debilitating when they are automatic and unconscious. There are times, to be sure, when our automated actions are right and proper—slamming on the brakes when the car in front of us unexpectedly slows down. But checking email again and again "for no good reason," or switching tasks when we feel bored or anxious—these are often circumstances when there is no *real* possibility of choice, when we're simply at the mercy of internal and external triggers, and when our habitual responses may well be unhealthy and unhelpful. Under such circumstances, a better response may be to *increase* the choices available to us, opening up the space of possibilities, so we can discover what else we might do. If we're bored, maybe we should get up and take a walk. Or maybe we should keep doing what we're doing, accepting boredom as a momentary companion as we carry on. If we're driving when we hear the sound of a new text message, maybe we should just keep driving, simply recognizing the anxiety and the "fear of missing out" that we now feel. Maybe we should pull over to the side of the road to read the text. Or maybe we should silence, or even turn off, our phone as soon as we get in the car.

At other times, our online choices may be debilitating when they are too plentiful. Then liberation may come from *reducing* our options. In the focused email exercise, for example, where the task is to do email and only email, some people discover that this is the case. Thus Krista says, "I noticed a degree of what I will call peace. It was a kind of peace brought on by a lack of alternatives. I guess I'll just attend to all of my email because that's what I can do." Similarly, Erin observes that she felt "relaxed and free—not pressed for time or rushing through anything." And in the multitasking exercises, some people see that they are more successful and happier when they minimize the number of tasks they are juggling.

The challenge, of course, is knowing when to increase the number of choices and when to reduce them. Sometimes it is obvious: don't text and drive. But most of the time, it is a matter of paying attention to the actual circumstances of our lives.

Taking Charge, Reducing Stress

When we are consciously exercising choice (or consciously choosing not to choose), we are taking control of our online lives, rather than responding passively to the circumstances that present themselves to us. Again and again in the reflections my students write, they talk about "control" and "agency" as qualities they have been learning to cultivate.

The first step is simply noticing that we don't have control and seeing how this affects us. Says Martin: "I learned that email, along with a host of other online distractions, is something that I need to get control over. It is a source of anxiety and also at the same time of scary ambivalence. The way that I can check it compulsively without awareness or emotion connected to it feels empty. I am also amazed by how it can quickly swing my emotions, notice how it can ramp up whatever emotion it is that I am feeling, especially if that emotion is under stress."

The next step is to discover what it will take to gain a greater measure of control. Often enough, just seeing the problem can get us a good distance toward a solution. Thus Martin concludes that "instead of letting my attention or the tasks control me, I can learn to pause, acknowledge the drift or pull on my attention, and let it go." And Will notices that exercising control through conscious choice reduces his stress: "Multitasking seems to become unpleasant when we kind of lose control of that decision-making ability. I certainly noticed that when I was able to decide what I wanted to do and was able to act on it there was a sense of freedom and less stress."

Will is right to notice the relationship between control and stress. Research clearly demonstrates the link. In *The End of Stress as We Know It*, Bruce McEwen, a leading stress researcher, points out, "In all of the research into stress, the concept of control appears again and again, the way a musical theme weaves in and out of the movements of a symphony. When stress is coupled with a lack of control, the music goes from major to minor." And, he adds, "control doesn't mean controlling others, telling people what to do, and generally being the top dog in the outfit; in an unstable environment the top dogs are likely to be the ones with the psychosomatic illness. Rather, it means control over one's own life."[3]

Sometimes we have sufficient control to change the objective circumstances of our lives. But even when we don't, we have the potential to change our relationship with, and our response to, the conditions that are stressing us out. "When we can't change our environment," McEwen says, "this is the time to change the things we can."[4]

Chronic stress, as we saw in Chapter 3, can take a serious toll on our bodies, leading in the most extreme cases to debilitating ailments and even death. Our bodies express the shock—might we even say the grief?—of living out of balance. So by paying attention to what our bodies are telling us, we're in a position to diagnose and respond. Sometimes, we can change the objective conditions. (If reading email in bed first thing in the morning stresses us out, maybe we should stop doing it.) Other times, we may be able to reduce the extent of the stress reaction, even if we can't eliminate the stressor. (When we're caught in a firestorm of online and offline activity, consciously relaxing the body may mitigate some of the stress.)

The breath, as we saw earlier, is a powerful tool for both diagnosis and intervention. It can tell us that we're in fight-or-flight mode. And a few moments of relaxed breathing may reduce the stress response. Indeed, attending to the breath (or to other sensations or body posture) can insert a pause into our unconscious forward movement, creating not only a moment of rest but a chance to pause and reassess. Pausing is one of the most important possibilities we can discover, for it can permit us to unhook, and thus to further cultivate a measure of control.

Pausing, Stopping, Resting

It can be quite painful to discover how hooked we've become to our digital lives. And for those of us who have previously noticed it, it can be painful to observe it more closely. There are many reasons why we're online for large stretches of time and find it difficult to unplug. Sometimes our work demands it of us. And to the extent that we've internalized the cultural message to be more "productive," to go ever faster and operate ever more efficiently, we may find it hard to disconnect, even when we can—or should. (Some of my students give voice to this, taking productivity simply as a fact of life, not a condition to be investigated and perhaps questioned. "Productivity is a martial art that I have spent years crafting," an undergraduate named Nick says proudly.)

Playtime and social interaction, of course, also exert their pull and hold us online, as much as does work. Often, taking a break from work means switching to other digital activities. And so our time online can appear to be a seamless web of activity, a mixture of work, play, and other activities not so easily classified. Emily puts it nicely when she says, "The hyperlinky world that we live in is remarkable and exciting, yet is really quite impossible because there are no start and finish lines anymore. I start reading something, and then click to read the added bonus information and click to watch a related video from there, and then am transported to completely unrelated videos, and I never make it back to the first piece—I haven't read any one thing in its entirety—and feel exhausted and like I failed."[5]

In a sense Emily is right: There are no more start and finish lines—although it might be better to say that the lines have been weakened rather than fully obliterated. The distinctions between the week and the weekend, between daytime and nighttime, between worktime and playtime are losing their force. But pausing and stopping are no less important in a world of seemingly endless online enticement and opportunity. Here it is worth remembering the Sabbath idea, which I mentioned in Chapter 8. As a Jewish institution, the Sabbath recognizes that we humans need to rest (the English word that corresponds to the Hebrew *shabbat*) as well as to work. Indeed, without adequate rest our work will often suffer. Thus do we need rest *for the sake of our work*. But the ancient understanding of the Sabbath, while acknowledging this fact, posits another, more radical reason for resting: *for the sake of our humanity*. The Sabbath, in this second conception, is a time to savor and appreciate our lives, to smell the flowers, literally and figuratively. We need time not just to do but to be.

Cultivating the ability to pause and to stop is a central concern in all the exercises. Sometimes, the pause is a momentary break in the flow of activity. We stop long enough to notice the emotion we're experiencing, thus disrupting the automated reaction that otherwise would have taken place. And as we accumulate moments of pausing and noticing, we begin to see patterns of behavior that were largely invisible when we were caught up in the doing. At other times in the exercises, the pause or stop is more substantial. We forgo certain online behaviors for hours or days in order to see how particular devices and apps may have hooked us. And in addition to pausing and noticing in these ways, we take the time to reflect on what we've seen, stepping outside our online activities and looking back at them.

Pausing and stopping, it turns out, are crucial both instrumentally and noninstrumentally. Instrumentally, they help us see how to operate online in healthier and more effective ways. Not only is it generally unproductive to stay online when we're distracted and tired, but our lack of physical mobility can create health problems that will further limit our productivity in the future. As Holly says, "I'm beginning to recognize internal triggers that signal for time out: stiff muscles, an awareness of jumping from one unrelated thought to another, feeling anxious and pressured to complete any given task." Getting up, moving around, and stretching is good for business.

But pausing and stopping can also help us recover and strengthen the noninstrumental dimension of our lives. For in disrupting our constant doing, pausing and stopping may shift us from what the psychologists Zindel Segal, Mark Williams, and John Teasdale call "driven mode" to "being mode." Being mode, they say, "is characterized by a sense of freedom, freshness, and unfolding of experience in new ways. It is responsive to the richness and complexity of the unique patterns that each moment presents." Whereas in driven mode, by contrast, "the multidimensional nature of experience is reduced primarily to a unidimensional analysis of its standing in relation to a goal state."[6] Here, for example, in his final reflection on the course, Henry notes the freedom, relaxation, and joy that he discovered during a Sabbath-like experience earlier in his life. The reading we had done in class on the idea of the Sabbath, he says,

> made me think more carefully about the place and value of Sabbath in our life and culture, and to remember back to Denmark, when very few stores—grocery stores included—were open on

Sunday. This small initial inconvenience quickly turned into a great source of pleasure for my friends and myself, as Sundays emerged as ideal days to stroll around exploring the city, watching others do the same. I began to think more about what it means to take a day completely off work, and to realize the differences between telling myself I will do no work on a Saturday, intending to do work and doing none, and doing even a little work (like checking email), and to realize the restorative nature of a full Sabbath. I began taking full days off (perhaps at least checking email), realizing the freedom and relaxation that can be felt with a simple refusal to do any work for a day (before the day even begins). I spent some of the days I did this relaxing, reading, running, and seeing friends, and quickly realized the joy that could come from taking a complete day off work.

Living Fast and Slow

When I first began studying calligraphy many years ago, it was as an explicit alternative to my digital pursuits. I felt the need to balance the heady, abstract work of computer science and artificial intelligence with the embodied, fluid gestures of a handcraft. As it turned out, my study of calligraphy served me well. It opened the door to more contemplative ways of being in the world. Although I first conceived of it as an escape from the Fast World, the big surprise was that calligraphy—and the other contemplative practices that followed, including meditation—also offered me guidance in living in the Fast World more artfully, in integrating Fast World and Slow World practices.

Another surprise was that my calligraphic studies offered me insights into what I will call the politics of craft. I was able to take up calligraphy in the 1970s because it had been revived three-quarters of a century earlier as part of the Arts and Crafts movement. This movement, which began in late-nineteenth-century England, aimed to recover the craft knowledge that had been lost during the previous century of industrialization. The broad popularity of handcrafts in the West today is largely the result of these efforts. (Even the term "arts and crafts" is a direct reference back to this movement.)

Yet few of us today realize that the movement was about more than creating beautiful things by hand: it was actually a political movement. Indeed, the craftwork undertaken by its members was intended as a direct response to, a reaction against, industrialization. They felt that the mechanization of society was dehumanizing people—at its worst turning people into machines. And they hoped to right this balance, bringing the hand and the body more fully back into daily life, and creating beautiful things.[7]

Any craft, of course, can be considered as a purely technical enterprise. Today you can take up calligraphy (or bookbinding, or spinning, or weaving) in exactly this way. The classes you take and the books you read on the subject will largely introduce you to the tools, materials, and techniques you need to create the beautiful things you aspire to make. In much the same spirit, you can explore how to improve your digital craft purely as a matter of technique. Indeed, the exercises in this book are largely constructed to further just this kind of exploration. But it is my hope that as you bring greater attention to your online life you also pay attention to the larger social and political context within which you are operating. In performing your digital craftwork, what values are you supporting and expressing?

For much of the digital era, it has been challenging to express public concerns about where our digital developments were taking us. And if you did, you were likely to be dismissed as a Luddite. (The term refers to an early-nineteenth-century movement that opposed the mechanization of the weaving industry in England. While the term today refers to someone who is considered to be antitechnology, the original Luddites weren't against mechanization per se but rather were against some of its economic and social effects.) In recent times, however, I have sensed a shift, a growing willingness to look at the pluses and minuses of our digital lives. I sense that we as a culture may be preparing to enter into a broader and deeper conversation about the place of all things digital in our lives. It is my hope that the ideas—and yes, the techniques—in this book, can contribute to that conversation. This is the subject of my concluding chapter.

10

Broadening and Deepening the Conversation

For ten years, I have been in conversation with undergraduates at colleges and universities around the country. The main topic has been their relationship with their digital tools. It all began in the fall of 2005 when I was teaching an introduction to information science to undergraduates at the University of Washington. I had created a short unit on quality of life in the digital age, and as part of this I thought it would be interesting to survey the sixty students on their uses of and their attitudes toward their digital devices and applications. I quickly put together a brief questionnaire that posed such questions as "Do you ever feel you spend too much time online, or plugged in to other media (music, cell phones, etc.)? Why or why not?"

I asked them to write their responses in class and to turn them in so I could review them before we met later that week. And since I was curious to get an immediate sense of their responses, I asked for a show of hands on several of the questions. "How many of you said you feel you spend too much time online?" I asked. I was surprised to see more than half the students raise their hands. "Oh really," I said. "Tell me more about it. What is it you're doing and why do you feel it's too much?" The room opened up as students began to talk energetically about the challenges they faced. They spoke about losing track of time while they were online and missing out on other activities they valued, about constantly checking email and MySpace without good reason, about how hard it was to disconnect even when they wanted to. The conversation was all the richer, and obviously real, because there was room for these people to express their concerns, and at the same time for others to express their enthusiastic and uncritical embrace of all things digital.

Back then (and still today, I believe) our cultural story was that those "born digital" not only were savvy users of the technologies but were also uniformly enthralled by them—as opposed to the dinosaurs in the older generation who didn't have the same skills or positive attitude. But here were young people giving voice to a wider range of views, which was all the more noteworthy because most of them weren't poets or history majors—they were headed for careers in the tech industry.

I wondered whether this was a unique circumstance. And so, as I was invited to other campuses to give lectures and workshops, I began to ask to serve as a guest lecturer in one or more undergraduate classes. In each class, I would ask students to fill out a version of the questionnaire, following which I would moderate a conversation about the questions. Typically, I would ask for a quick show of hands on a couple of the main questions, so that students could see how their classmates had responded. Over the past ten years I have made appearances in courses on a wide range of subjects—English, psychology, communications, computer and information science, business, social work, and so on—and the results have been the same. Many of the students express concerns about their relationship with their digital tools. Indeed, in recent years nearly all students say they spend too much time online, and those who don't, when asked, say that they've made changes to reduce the amount of time they're online and to increase the quality of their interactions. (Yet at the same time, these students make it clear that they appreciate their digital tools and their online lives. They aren't Luddites.) What's more, the quality of the conversation is invariably high—the students are thoughtful and articulate, and they are enthusiastically engaged. They clearly want to have this conversation.

I draw two conclusions from all this. First, we need to be careful about the assumptions we make about people's relationship to the digital world. I am convinced that our current story about the differences between digital natives and their parents and grandparents is wrong (although I certainly wouldn't claim that I have the definitive proof). Digital natives aren't monolithically the same, and we might wonder what social and political purposes are being served when we claim that they are. Second, we have an opportunity to engage one another, both within and across generations, in a broader and deeper conversation. We have much to tell one another, and to learn from one another, once we create the conditions for genuine discussion and dialogue.[1]

Is Google Making Us Stupid?

The conversation about our digital lives is of course happening all around us, and in a variety of ways many of us are participating in it. We talk about the latest iPhone release and the latest cool apps. We speculate about the fate of the Silicon Valley giants, such as Facebook, Google, and Microsoft, and about the trajectory of recent start-ups. We show off our latest digital acquisitions while also complaining about how overloaded we are. We wonder (and at times worry) about what the Internet is doing to our brains, about whether privacy is passé (and whether this matters), about whether e-books will take the place of printed books, and about how digital technologies will affect education (for better or worse).

This last group of speculations interests me the most, because within and behind them I hear echoes of some of our deepest questions. What do all these digital changes *mean?* And what do they mean *for me* (as well as for my family, for my social group, for humanity, and for the planet)? We don't have the definitive studies that would answer such questions—and it isn't clear whether we ever will. In the meanwhile, much of the public conversation is dominated by debates among experts and pundits that is severely constrained by today's sound bite–limited modes of public communication, as well as by overbroad generalizations.

Consider the faceoff that took place in 2010 between Nicholas Carr and Clay Shirky on the op-ed pages of the *Wall Street Journal.* The journalist Carr had just published his book *The Shallows: What the Internet Is Doing to Our Brains,* an expansion of his lead story in the *Atlantic,* "Is Google Making Us Stupid?" And Shirky, the media specialist at New York University known for his belief in the redemptive powers of the Internet, was asked to respond. Each had roughly twelve hundred words to answer the question, "Does the Internet make you smarter or dumber?"[2]

The Internet is making us dumber, Carr asserted. "With its constant distractions and interruptions," he said, it "is turning us into scattered and superficial thinkers." We no longer live in a culture of the book, a technology that once trained the mind to focus. Naturally,

Shirky took the opposite position. Sure, he said, there is plenty to distract us on the Internet, but changes in media always initially produce a certain amount of junk, until new institutional models of quality help us sort the wheat from the chaff. We will work this out, just as we have in the past, and the linking of billions of people via digital media will ultimately allow us to tap our "cognitive surplus" in order to "create enormous positive effects."

These two men are smart, educated, and knowledgeable, and each of them makes valuable points. Yet in reading their essays, which I regularly assign in my classes as a conversation starter, I am struck less by the force of their arguments than by two assumptions that they share. The first is that there is a single black-and-white answer to the question they are debating: *Either* the Internet is making us smarter *or* it is making us dumber. The second is that the changes they identify are inevitable: The emergence of the Internet will *necessarily* bring about these great (or terrible) things.

It doesn't take much reflection to realize that these positions are somewhat suspect—or at least open to further consideration. Why shouldn't the Internet make us smarter *in some ways* and dumber *in others?* Besides, who is "us"? Isn't it likely that the helpful and unhelpful aspects of Internet use will vary with culture and education and so on? And what do we mean by smart and dumb, anyway? Furthermore, what reason is there to think that what happened before will necessarily happen again, or that certain effects of media are inevitable? Shouldn't we be asking why someone thinks a certain outcome is inevitable, and shouldn't we wonder whether the argument for inevitability is meant to disarm our impulse to intervene? (Isn't the claim for inevitability one of the strategies that stops people from going to the voting booth?)

As should now be clear, like Nicholas Carr I worry about the effects of distraction, mindless acceleration, and the loss of attentional acuity. But unlike him, I don't think the Internet is the "cause," nor do I think that this trend need continue. Neither do I agree with Clay Shirky that good things will inevitably come to us through the Internet because that's the way media change inevitably happens. Rather, as I have demonstrated in this book, we have an opportunity to cultivate habits and practices of mind and body that can encourage us to make good use of the new technologies—and that can help us discuss and determine just what "good use" might mean. How things turn out will depend *on us,* and on what we do or don't do. It isn't foreordained.

Beyond Smart or Stupid

An important dimension of the human developmental process is the discovery that we are all complex creatures, each with lovely qualities as well as not so lovely qualities. Simply in virtue of our humanity, we are capable of being warm and loving, compassionate, and altruistic. At the same time, unavoidably, we are capable of acting out of hate, spite, and envy. Yet when we fail to recognize our own so-called dark side, we are likely to project these unlovely qualities onto others, onto individuals as well as onto entire social groups. Thus the "enemy" becomes the embodiment of all that is evil while we ourselves are the opposite, the embodiment of all that is good. (Naturally, our enemies feel the same way about us.)

Similarly, I've come to believe, we are more likely to approach our relationship to all things digital (or to any other issue we care deeply about) in simplistic terms—good or bad, smart or stupid—when we fail to see the complexity of our own views. But when we can look more closely and honestly at how we relate to our digital tools and practices, we're more likely to see greater complexity, noticing that our attitudes and behaviors depend upon our moods, the time of day we're online, what we're trying to accomplish at the moment, and so on. Sometimes we may even notice ambivalence, that we hold conflicting and contradictory feelings and attitudes.

Over the years, I've noticed how I both do and don't want new email. I am always hoping that something wonderful, maybe even transcendent, will show up in my little inbox. Rarely does this happen, of course, and I am disappointed. Moreover, whatever has arrived will mean more work for me, if not a response at least a decision to file or delete it. But even when something wonderful (or nice enough) comes along, it still can't match the exaggerated hope that is embedded in my decision to check for new mail. So I smile when I notice similar sentiments being expressed by my students, as Diane does here: "When I went to consciously check email my state of mind was usually one of worry," she says. "I didn't notice holding my breath when first checking, but I did notice disappointment when I didn't have a new email, and annoyance when I did. It was as if I wanted communication, but when I received it I was annoyed at having to respond. The tension between desire for communication and connection to others and the want to be 'not busy' and to be alone was something that came up a lot, and I'm not sure if it's ever something that I will be able to reconcile." I appreciate such insights not only because I happen to share them, but because I appreciate the careful observation and honest articulation that they represent.

And I love it when students not only notice the complexity but also recognize that the process we've been through together has helped them to see it, as Samantha does here:

> At the end of our last class discussion, David, you described our relationship with technology as "complex, contradictory, and changing." I know, for me personally, that this is very true. I often feel conflicted about my technology use, because there are times when I get a lot of enjoyment and satisfaction out of it—like when I'm Face-timing with my sister or someone "likes" my post on Facebook. Sometimes this enjoyment is rather shallow, but I don't think that's necessarily a bad thing. Other times, I feel immensely frustrated by my technologies, because I feel obligated to keep up (which seems like an impossible task) and I sometimes do this at the expense of higher-priority activities. And up until recently, I would get frustrated but I wouldn't stop myself or change any-thing about my technology use. Now I know that I can change my behavior and I'm not obligated to continue doing something that isn't working or that makes me unhappy. On some level, it seems like I should have already known this but I don't think I was aware of my feelings/actions enough to recognize what I needed.

By seeing that at times we love our digital tools and our digital lives and at other times despair of them, and by seeing when and why these attitudes manifest themselves, I suspect that we are less likely to claim that the Internet, or email, or Facebook, or multitasking is simply good or simply bad, that it is saving or ruining us. And when we can bring this more nuanced self-understanding to discussion with others, we may be able to grant to them the right to hold different (and equally complex) opinions. This is what happens in the classroom, and it leads to a much richer and more fulfilling discussion. Can we at least imagine such a possibility in our more public forums?

Creating the Conditions for a Deeper Conversation

If we are to have such conversations, trust, respect, and sincere listening must also be present. For if we are to talk honestly about the place of the technologies in our lives, and to give voice to our own uncertainty and confusion, we need to feel that what we say will be heard and respected. Otherwise, we will refuse to speak at this level of disclosure, and our discussions will degenerate into arguments dominated by strong emotions.

In my course I work hard, from the very first week, to create a safe, nonjudgmental environment in which anything the students discover about the technologies or themselves—good or bad, seemingly obvious, wrong, or controversial—is fair game to acknowledge and to say. It is an environment in which students are free—indeed, encouraged—to make provisional observations and to speculate about what they are seeing without feeling that they have to present definitive proof or a fully worked out articulation of what they are experiencing. Danielle acknowledges this when she says that as result of the course, "I am better equipped to have these conversations, explain my position, be more open to other's views (that I may agree with, or not, or am not sure), and continue to explore this theme and not feel overwhelmed, anxious, or terrified if I do not fully understand a topic or have a set position. So often I think we are asked to have an opinion or a 'take' before we have had proper time to consider a topic. One aspect of critical thinking that I have been able to further develop in this class is being comfortable with not having an opinion or being able to change my stance once I have seen more research on a topic."

Chances are good, I also tell my students, that at some point during the course they will be triggered by something we've read or something someone has said. Many of us have strong feelings about the place of the digital in our lives, and we can become upset when one of our deeply held beliefs is challenged. This can happen, I've observed over the years, at any point in the course. But I've noticed that it comes up particularly strongly and consistently when we talk about addiction—about whether there is such a thing as addiction to digital apps and devices. For the past few years, I have invited Hilarie Cash to class to lead a session on Internet and video game addiction. Hilarie is a clinical psychologist who is the cofounder of the reSTART Internet Addiction Recovery Program, whose mission is to assist people "with an Internet and/or computer based behavioral problem." Although the subject is still being debated in the scientific literature (see my remarks in Appendix E), Hilarie strongly asserts her position: that people can and do become addicted, in the clinical sense, to the Internet and to video games. Each time she has come to class, the room heats up with people's strong reactions—especially from those students who are resistant to Hilarie's point of view.[3]

So I prepare my students for such times, beginning the very first week, telling them that these moments will inevitably arise. I suggest that such moments, rather than being "problems," will be learning opportunities: for the students who have been triggered to see what is arising and to work with it, and for the rest of us to be supportive (and to

the extent possible to avoid being dragged unconsciously into the up-
heaval). Weathering these situations successfully, I've observed, further
cements the sense of trust and safety. We really can handle challenges in
respectful ways that further our individual and collective learning.

I sometimes assign a short article from the *New York Times* (in
other courses I teach as well) from 2006, written by the science journalist Benedict Carey. It reports how neuroscientists have tracked "what
happens in the politically partisan brain when it tries to digest damning
facts about favored candidates or criticisms of them." What the experi-
menters found was that subjects were more likely to respond favorably
to positions they already held and to reject positions that contradicted
their own. (This should hardly be surprising.) More interesting was
that when they were rejecting positions that were unacceptable to
them, brain centers primarily concerned with emotion were active, not
those associated with reasoning. The subjects were emotionally rejecting what they were already predisposed to discount, not responding
thoughtfully to it. At the end of the article, Drew Westen, the lead author of the study, is quoted saying that it is possible to override these
largely unconscious reactions, "but you have to engage in ruthless self
reflection, to say, 'All right, I know what I want to believe, but I have to
be honest.'"[4]

Getting beyond unconscious reactions through honest self-
reflection—this is, of course, central to the work we have been exploring in this book. Learning to recognize triggers, to pause, and then to
respond skillfully can help us improve our relationship with our digital
tools. These very same skills can be applied in the classroom, and potentially in any communal situation, especially when a sense of safety,
trust, and respect is being cultivated.

Establishing Shared Norms and Conventions

All of this work, as I indicated in the first chapter, places the focus on the individual: the discoveries that each of us can make for ourselves, and the changes we can institute in our own individual behavior. Focusing on ourselves as individuals is valuable—indeed, it is the place in our lives where we generally have the greatest leverage. But it is by no means the whole story. We are social creatures with responsibilities to others and to the world. Not all choices are up to us individually. How can we come to decisions about norms, rules, and guidelines governing the collective use of digital technologies—decisions that may well place limits on what individuals can and can't do?

Earlier I noted one such example: deciding whether and how to regulate the use of digital devices while driving. In this particular instance we can see that American society has been moving toward a widely shared agreement that the use of such devices ought to be banned or at least severely limited. Here the growing scientific evidence (that the use of digital devices in the car is as distracting as driving drunk) has combined with an awareness of the possible consequences (injury and even death). Although it has taken years to reach this consensus, and the consensus isn't (yet) universal, I consider this to be the easy case. There really does appear to be a right answer.

The harder cases are those in which there may not be a single right answer—right, that is, for all individuals, or for all communities, at all times. One such example is the use of digital devices in the classroom or in a business meeting. Many of us have found ourselves in such settings, and we know how it generally goes. Laptops are open (and phones are sometimes out and active, as well). If you are the speaker, you can feel the diminished attention in the room as people's faces are buried in their devices. If you are a listener, you may be doing your best to split your attention between the speaker and your email (say), and you may actually believe that you are doing a pretty good job of it. Or you may acknowledge that your attention is mainly directed to your online tasks, but at least you're there (you may tell yourself) and can shift your attention to the speaker when the need arises. But if you believe, as I do, that attention and learning are *coconstructed,* that the quality of speaking and listening (and therefore learning and engagement) are the product of what the group is and is not doing, then situations like this are far from ideal, unless you've set the bar quite low for what you hope to achieve. What can be done?

The choices are clear, at least in outline. You can ban the use of all devices, refrain from setting a use policy, or place some restrictions on the use of the devices. Banning the devices (assuming you have the authority to do so) has its problems. The devices certainly have legitimate uses in both the classroom and the meeting room: for reading and writing, and for task-appropriate information seeking and research. Setting no use policy, thus allowing the participants to make their own decisions, has its problems, too. It not only allows but may actually encourage the individual to redirect his or her attention elsewhere. And this will have consequences not only for the individual but for the whole group (since those wanting to pay attention to the content of the class or meeting are often distracted by their neighbors). The third option, placing limits on use, may just open the door to unrestricted use. (At the end of a course I taught a couple of years ago, where I permitted students to use their laptops for note-taking and reading but asked them not to venture onto the Internet, a student told me privately that she wished I'd banned the use of laptops in the classroom. Why? I asked. Because once her laptop was open, she explained, she couldn't stop herself from checking email.)

I have tried all these approaches in the classroom. I don't feel that any one of them is necessarily or always best (but see Clay Shirky's reasoning in recently deciding to ban all devices in *his* classrooms).[5] What I have concluded, however, is that the work of self-observation and group discussion can play a valuable role whatever decision is made. Let me illustrate with an actual example.

Each year I teach a required course in one of the Information School's master's programs. I generally permit students to use their laptops and tablets in the classroom (but not their phones) and ask them, on the honor system, not to wander off to email, Facebook, and the like. (It was in this course that the student told me she wished I'd banned laptops.) I also tell them that seeing students hiding behind their laptop screens (which is how it sometimes appears to me) reduces my concentration and affects the quality of my teaching. Don't they want me to be the most effective teacher I can be, for their sake? So I tell them my preference is that they don't use their laptops in class unless it's important for their own learning—and if they do use them, that they lower their laptop lids when they're not actively using the device.

This has always had mixed results. Some people can't help straying beyond the classroom content (like the student I've mentioned), and others either forget about the restrictions or don't feel constrained by them. Some regularly forget to lower their laptop lids. On the other hand, some choose not to use their devices at all, either because it's their preference or because they want to honor mine, and some use their devices completely in keeping with the guidelines I've established—because they want to and they have the attentional strength to achieve this.

Last year I decided to try something new in this course. I decided to make the use of digital devices in the classroom an explicit topic and to import some of the elements from my course on Information and Contemplation—specifically self-observation, reflection, and discussion. In the first class session I explained that I hadn't yet settled on a policy regarding the use of devices in the classroom, and in the first few weeks we would experiment with different policies (no devices, limited use of devices, anything goes) and I would survey the class to see how they felt about the different policies. We would talk about the results and at the end of the process I would announce a policy, taking into account what we had discovered, as well as my own preferences.

So what happened? For me, the single biggest result had to do with people's overall preferences. More than half of the forty-student cohort had a personal preference for no tech in the classroom. Yet when I asked them whether they wanted to impose this policy on the class, a number of them said no. They felt that other members of the class had the right to use their devices for legitimate classroom purposes. Other students, of course, did express a preference for devices in the classroom—mostly for limited tech use, some for unrestricted use. But these students didn't express concern for their classmates who preferred no tech. In fact, several adopted an aggressive attitude: They'll just have to get used to all the technologies around them. In the vote on which policy to adopt, the limited-tech policy won, and I decided to adopt it, essentially settling upon the very policy that I had used in the past. Yet I was fairly certain that students' behavior would now be informed and affected by the process we'd been through. And had I decided to adopt the no-tech option, which I still may do in the future, my guess is that the class would have better understood it and been prepared to treat it as a legitimate form of learning and experimentation, even though not everyone liked it.

I make no claim about the generalizability of these particular results. But I present them in the context of a process that I do believe is generalizable: a process of experimentation, observation, and reflection that can help us learn more about our relationship with our digital tools and open up a broader and deeper conversation. While I don't think that this exact process would work in, say, corporate meetings, it isn't hard to imagine variants on it that might work in such settings, especially at a time when industry and nonprofits have recognized that how their employees use their digital tools can easily affect productivity and health.

When the Means Are Also the End

To pay attention, to be more mindful or aware, is to be more intimately connected with what is going on within and around us. (The word "intimate" in its origins means "made known," and when we are intimate with someone or something, we are close enough to that person or thing to have a personal relationship with it, and to care.) Using the language of intimacy, we might say that this book has been about establishing a more intimate—a more careful and caring—relationship with and through our digital tools and devices. Through mindful observation and reflection, we demonstrate that we care enough to improve this relationship.

Intimacy shows up in another way as well in this work. For two decades, I have been bringing people together to talk about the place of digital technologies in their lives. I have done this in my courses, but also through various workshops and conferences that I have held around the country. In all these instances, it has been important to establish an atmosphere of honesty, trust, and respect, and to encourage people to express what was on their hearts and minds. What I have discovered along the way is quite simple: When we talk about the technologies, we are ultimately talking about our lives, and about their meaning and value. And when we come together to have caring and careful conversations about the place of the technologies, we establish an intimacy of connection that many of us long for. What thus seems like an instrumental step—the attempt to figure out how to use the technologies to improve our lives—turns out to produce what we are hoping for: the means are also the end. Thus our digital technologies can bring us together in a way that hasn't yet been much noticed or discussed: The *conversations* about their place in our lives can lead us to richer exchanges and more caring connections.

How do we do this? My hope, of course, is that people will undertake the exploratory exercises in this book, both in groups and by themselves. But these exercises—as much as I love them and stand by them—are only *examples,* which are meant to demonstrate the power and possibility that self-observation and reflection open up. There are so many other ways to take this work forward, once you have understood the basic principles at work. An hourlong group conversation, carefully constructed, is enough to begin the process, as my opening remarks in this chapter were meant to suggest. Why not begin the conversation in your classroom, with your work group or church group or meditation group, with your family. Like me, you may be surprised by what you hear, and inspired and humbled by what you learn.

Appendix A
Two Attention-Training Practices

In the exercises in this book you are learning to strengthen both your task attention (so you can stay focused on whatever you are trying to accomplish) and your self-observational ability (so you're better able to notice what is happening in your mind and body while you're doing whatever you're doing).

Mindful Breathing

Box A.1 summarizes the mindful breathing practice, which can help you to develop stronger task focus. As I explain to my students, this practice is simple but not easy. *It is simple:* You begin to focus your attention on the sensations of your breathing (the in-and-out movements that arise as the lungs take in and expel air). And when you notice that your attention has wandered away to something else, you bring it back to the breath. But *it isn't easy:* Because the mind has a strong tendency to wander, we need to be patient, bringing our attention back again and again.

You needn't practice mindful breathing to do the work in this book. As I explain at the end of Chapter 3, you will actually be achieving some of the same results in Exercise 2, by bringing your attention

Box A.1: Mindful Breathing

Adopt a posture that is both relaxed and alert
For example: Sit upright in a chair, feet firmly on the ground, hands folded in your lap, eyes either closed or lightly open.

Begin attending to the sensations of your breathing
Identify a place in your body (your belly, your chest, your nostrils) where you can feel the physical sensations that arise as you breathe in and out.

Notice when your mind wanders away from the sensations of the breath
Inevitably, you will lose touch with the breath. When this happens, briefly notice where your attention has gone (to future planning, to a memory of an event from years ago, to an imagined dialogue with a friend?).

Bring your attention back to the breath
Once you've noticed that your mind has wandered, return to the sensations of the breath. However many times your mind wanders away, just keep bringing it back.

back to your email when you find yourself wandering away. Still, mindful breathing is one of the simplest practices you can do to strengthen your attention. (I do a version of it every morning.) My students sometimes find it helpful to take ten or fifteen minutes for mindful breathing before they go online.

There is also a variant of the exercise that is both simple and easy. All you need to do, at any moment of the day, is to take two or three conscious breaths: simply focus on the in-and-out movement of the breath, making an effort at the same time to relax your body. It's easy: who can't sustain their attention on their breathing for two, three, or four breaths? The hard part is remembering to do it.

The Mindful Check-in

In our rushed and production-oriented culture, we tend to be focused on "getting things done." This often means focusing more on the goal we're trying to achieve than on our actual moment-to-moment experience while we're working toward it. The mindful check-in practice is meant to counter this tendency, asking you to notice what is happening in your mind and body while you're online. As explained in Box A.2, it asks you to explore your breath and body, your emotional state, and the quality of your attention. (The actual order of the questions isn't as important as taking each one in turn, dwelling on each one long enough to see what you can discover about your current state of being.)

When I introduce this exercise in the classroom, I present it as a guided meditation, asking students initially to close their eyes, if they're comfortable doing so. I then pose each question in turn, giving them several minutes to answer it. The best way to understand this practice

Box A.2: The Mindful Check-in

What is the quality of your breathing?
    What is the quality of your breathing: Is it shallow or deep,
    fast or slow? Are you holding your breath?

What is going on in and with your body?
    What is your posture like (are you upright, slouched, or lying
    down)? Where do you feel tension or pain? Are parts of your
    body numb?

What is your current emotional state?
    Are you feeling up or down, excited, bored, anxious, . . . ?

What is the quality of your attention?
    Is your attention highly focused, or scattered, or somewhere
    in between?

is of course to do it, and so I suggest that you take a few minutes to
answer these questions for yourself right now, as you're reading these
words.

   What is the quality of your breathing? Take a moment to notice the
current rhythm and pattern of your breathing, but don't try to alter it
(although some change may naturally occur during this period of observation). Is your breathing currently fast or slow, shallow or deep?

Are you holding your breath? Or are you perhaps having trouble even noticing your breathing?

What is going on in and with your body? How are you sitting, standing, or lying down? Are you holding yourself in a comfortable position? Can you notice places of tension or pain (in your neck or shoulders, for example), or places where you are currently numb to sensation? Overall, would you say that you are feeling relaxed or tense?

What is your current emotional state? You may find a word to describe your current state, such as "delighted" or "bored." Or trying to find a verbal label may get in the way of just sensing your current mood. Then too, you may not be able to identify your emotional state, either verbally or nonverbally. In this case, does the quality of your breathing or the state of your body (which you examined in the first two questions) give you any hints about your current emotional state?

What is the quality of your attention? How focused or distracted are you at the moment? Answering the three previous questions may have been hard because it has been challenging to focus on them, and thus to pay attention to your breath, your body, and your emotions. (If this is the case, just knowing this, recognizing the current state of your attention, is itself an achievement.) Or you may be in a state of greater settled and focused awareness.

The mindful check-in can be done just as I've outlined it here, as you sequence through these questions over the course of a few minutes. But after you've gained some familiarity with the process of turning your attention inward in this way, it can also be done in a more abbreviated form: You simply ask yourself, "How am I feeling right now?" and notice which aspects of your current mental and bodily experience are most salient.

Appendix B
A Template for Logging Your Observations

In Step 3 of each of the exercises, you are asked to log (to take notes on) what you observe while you're engaged in the exercise's "primary practice" (using email, multitasking, or unplugging). While you are welcome to create your own format for this log, I offer you a starting point on the following page.

Your name:

Exercise you performed:

Start time	End time	What were you doing?	What was your experience?	What does this suggest?

Appendix C
Contemplative Pedagogy

Considerable work is now going on around the country and across the globe to bring contemplative practices and perspectives into education—to create contemplative pedagogy. For those wanting to learn more about this movement, I can suggest several organizations that will serve as entry points, whether your focus is on higher education or on K–12 education.

Contemplative Practices in Higher Education

One national organization primarily has spearheaded the incorporation of contemplative practices into higher education, the Center for Contemplative Mind in Society, which has been in existence for nearly twenty years. (I am on the board of the Center and was a recipient of one of its fellowships.) The Center has spawned an academic society, the Association for Contemplative Mind in Higher Education (ACMHE), which sponsors an annual academic conference and an academic journal.

The Center's Web site is a good starting point for learning more about current directions in contemplative pedagogy in higher education. The Web site maintains links to the ACMHE, its journal, and its conference, as well as to various resources, including books, articles, and webinars. Members of the ACMHE can join an active listserv where participants regularly discuss practices and pedagogy, and announce new publications and upcoming events.[1]

Contemplative Practices in K–12 Education

In K–12 education, there has been an explosion of books, programs, and institutions concerned with contemplation and mindfulness. I will mention two organizations that can provide an entryway to this work (although both organizations welcome those who are involved in higher education). The Association for Mindfulness in Education (AME) maintains a Web site with links to books and CDs, events, research, schools, and educational programs. The Mindfulness in Education Network (MiEN) also maintains a Web site with various resources, including video of presentations at its recent conferences. (I am on the board of MiEN.) Both AME and MiEN sponsor annual conferences and maintain active listservs.[2]

Appendix D
The Mindful Use of Technology

There are a number of resources and initiatives today that are exploring the relationship between the contemplative dimension of life and the digital world.

In *The Digital Distraction,* Alex Soojung-Kim Pang calls his approach to the blending of the digital and the contemplative "contemplative computing." The opening chapter of Howard Rheingold's *Net Smart: How to Thrive Online* is devoted to attention and distraction. "Are you captain or captive of your attention muscles?" Rheingold asks. Rafael Calvo and Dorian Peters include a chapter on mindfulness in their book, *Positive Computing.* And in his book *Wisdom 2.0,* Soren Gordhamer recounts his own struggles with digital "addiction"—how he came to acknowledge "the lack and incompleteness when I was not on my computer or my cell"—and his subsequent embrace of contemplative practices as an antidote.[1]

We are also beginning to see training programs, conferences, and digital apps that explore this territory. Google's internal training program, "Search Inside Yourself," has received considerable attention for introducing mindfulness to one of Silicon Valley's corporate powerhouses. Chade-Meng Tan, the originator of the program, has written a book, *Search Inside Yourself,* and has also spun off an independent

corporate training program, the Search Inside Yourself Leadership Institute. Soren Gordhamer, author of *Wisdom 2.0,* has also founded a
conference series with the same name. Meetings, which feature both
technologists and contemplatives as speakers, are held in the United
States and abroad. And there are a growing number of smart phone
apps that promote meditation and mindfulness.[2]

Appendix E
Digital Dependency and Addiction

We have all heard friends, classmates, or colleagues say that they are addicted to some device or app, or they know someone who is. We may have said it about ourselves. What we seem to mean when we use the word in this way is that the "addicted" person is a heavy user and is unhelpfully or unhealthily dependent on that device or app. The person in question finds it hard to stay off email or Facebook, or spends an inordinate amount of time playing video games, or can't go anywhere without his or her phone.

Apart from these common ways of talking, however, the scientific community has developed its own understanding of addiction as a clinical phenomenon, which isn't the same as the everyday references we so often make. What's more, scientists and clinicians are now engaged in a debate about whether there is such a thing as a digital addiction. The focus has been on the problematic use, the abuse, of video games and, more generally, the Internet. Two clinical diagnoses have been proposed: Internet Gaming Disorder and Internet Addiction Disorder.

Internet Gaming Disorder (IGD): The American Psychiatric Association (APA) lists Internet Gaming Disorder in the most recent edition of its diagnostic manual (the Diagnostic and Statistical Manual of

Mental Disorders, or DSM-V). In a fact sheet, the APA identifies IGD as "a condition warranting more clinical research and experience before it might be considered for inclusion in the main book as a formal disorder." The jury, in other words, is still out. The same fact sheet gives a brief, informal description of the phenomenon: "Recent scientific reports have begun to focus on the preoccupation some people develop with certain aspects of the Internet, particularly online games. The 'gamers' play compulsively, to the exclusion of other interests, and their persistent and recurrent online activity results in clinically significant impairment or distress. People with this condition endanger their academic or job functioning because of the amount of time they spend playing. They experience symptoms of withdrawal when pulled away from gaming."[1]

Internet Addiction Disorder (IAD): One succinct definition of Internet Addiction Disorder is "the inability of individuals to control their Internet use, resulting in marked distress and/or functional impairment in daily life." In 2012, the American Psychiatric Association proposed that a condition called Internet Use Disorder be included in the DSM-V and treated like IGD, as warranting further study. Criteria for identifying the condition included withdrawal symptoms when the Internet is taken away, and continued, excessive use despite "negative psychosocial problems." The proposal was not accepted, and there is no mention of Internet addiction in the DSM-V.[2]

Critics of these conditions make two arguments. The first has to do with the nature of addiction itself. The scientific community takes unhealthy dependence on substances, such as drugs and alcohol, as the primary (and possibly the only) form of addiction. There is a long-standing debate about whether there is such a thing as a behavioral, as opposed to a chemical, addiction—whether one can be addicted to an activity, such as shopping or sex. (As one critic says, behavioral addiction "is a problematic construct, as it implies that any behavior that is rewarding can be addictive.") Addiction to video games or the Internet would surely count as a behavioral addiction. Granting that behavioral addictions may exist, the second argument takes issue with the nature of the addiction. Critics say that one can't be addicted to the Internet, which is merely the medium or the delivery mechanism through which specific problematic activities are engaged. Instead, "Internet addiction should be replaced by addictions to specific online activities," such as shopping or pornography.[3]

No one in this debate seems to be denying that people can get into serious psychological trouble through their use of digital devices and apps. But there can be significant consequences resulting from how these discussions and debates, which are largely internal to the scientific and clinical communities, are resolved. Professional treatment follows from diagnosis, and the scope of the problem will depend on how the conditions are defined. (Estimates of the extent of Internet addiction in the United States vary widely, pointing to the current problem in defining and measuring the phenomenon.)[4]

I have no idea how the professional community will resolve these debates. But I can tell you how I approach the subject of addiction in my own work. Whether or not behavioral dependence should be considered addiction, I have no doubt that some people become dependent on their digital devices or apps in ways that are deeply dysfunctional. But extreme cases of addiction or dependency haven't thus far shown up in my world. (Could it be that some students or working adults I encounter are dangerously dependent? Yes, of course. But I have yet to be told about it—although people will sometimes tell me that someone they know had or has been exhibiting signs of serious dependence.) Instead, what I hear, quite regularly, are people's descriptions of their difficulty in letting go of some digital device, app, or practice. (You have seen many examples of this in this book, and may well have noticed it in yourself.) Someday, science may determine conclusively that the same brain mechanisms involved in chemical addiction are at work in behavioral dependence. Moreover, the science may show that these mechanisms are at work in lesser forms of dependence—when I check email many times a day despite feeling that it is an unnecessary and even unproductive practice. But for these lesser forms—the kind that we have been exploring in this book—I don't believe that we need a scientific explanation of the phenomena. What we need is honest observation, a commitment to make changes in the service of greater health, and the caring support of others around us.

Notes

Preface

1. Friedman, *Lexus and the Olive Tree*, 41.
2. See the article on the course that appeared in the *Chronicle of Higher Education*, Parry, "You're Distracted."

1. Falling in the Fountain

1. Try searching on the phrase "woman falls in fountain at mall." Several versions of the video are available online, as well as several incidents in which people fall into a pool or fountain.
2. Jobs, "Find What You Love."
3. Richtel, "Driven to Distraction"; Richtel, *A Deadly Wandering;* Richtel, "Texting While Driving."

3. Attention, Emotions, and the Body

1. James, *The Principles of Psychology*, 403–404. Studies of attention and popular introductions to the subject have multiplied in recent years. Daniel Goleman's recent book, *Focus: The Hidden Driver of Excellence,* is a readable introduction to the topic. I refer to his account several times in this chapter, sometimes supplementing his remarks with further studies.

2. In a review article for neuroscientists, "Attention Regulation and Monitoring in Meditation" (163), Lutz et al. distinguish between focused attention ("the focusing of attention on a chosen object") and open monitoring (the "nonreactive monitoring of the content of experience from moment to moment").

3. Discussion of the top-down and bottom-up systems can be found in Goleman, *Focus*, 24–38.

4. Ibid., 40.

5. "Under most conditions," says David Meyer, a psychologist who studies attention at the University of Michigan, "the brain simply cannot do two complex tasks at the same time. It can happen only when the two tasks are both very simple and when they don't compete with each other for the same mental resources. An example would be folding laundry and listening to the weather report on the radio. . . . But listening to a lecture while texting, or doing homework and being on Facebook—each of these tasks is very demanding, and each of them uses the same area of the brain, the prefrontal cortex." Quoted in Paul, "You'll Never Learn!" A good description of the orienting, alerting, and conflict-resolution functions can be found in Jha, Krompinger, and Baime, "Mindfulness Training Modifies Subsystems," 110.

6. There are also strong suggestions that multitasking negatively affects learning and memory. See the summary in Paul, "You'll Never Learn!" of recent research on multitasking as it applies to student learning. Clay Shirky, the New York University media scholar, in a blog post explaining why he has banned digital devices from the classroom, writes: "We've known for some time that multitasking is bad for the quality of cognitive work, and is especially punishing of the kind of cognitive work we ask of college students." Shirky, too, cites some of the relevant research. Shirky, "Why I Just Asked."

7. Sapolsky, "Stress, Stress-Related Disease," 609. An excellent introduction to the science of stress is *The End of Stress* by Bruce McEwen and Elizabeth Norton Lasley.

8. Goleman, *Emotional Intelligence;* Goleman, *Social Intelligence.*

9. Proponents of "embodied cognition" in philosophy, psychology, and linguistics argue that the body is crucial for understanding the nature of mind and cognition. Wilson and Foglia, "Embodied Cognition." Popular accounts describing the complex interrelationship between mind and body include Blakeslee and Blakeslee, *Mind of Its Own.*

10. Levine, *Get Up.*

11. Reynolds, "How Exercise Could Lead"; Laird and Strout, "Emotional Behaviors," 54–64.

12. Linda Stone, "Just Breathe."

13. Much of this work lies at the intersection of cognitive psychology, neuroscience, and clinical practice. Jon Kabat-Zinn's mindfulness-based stress reduction programs (MBSR), developed more than thirty years ago, have demonstrated that mindfulness meditation, yoga, and body awareness can improve people's ability to deal with stress and illness, in some cases even speeding up physical healing. Kabat-Zinn, *Full Catastrophe Living.* The scientific literature on the value of meditation as a form of attention training and emotion regulation has been exploding in recent years. For an overview see Ricard, Lutz, and Davidson, "Mind of the Meditator," 39–45.

14. James, *The Principles of Psychology,* 424.

4. Exercise 1

1. Yates, *Control Through Communication,* 96.

2. The Radicati Group, *Email Statistics Report, 2014–2018.* An article in the *Harvard Business Review* suggests that half of workers' time is spent managing email. Gill, "E-Mail: Not Dead, Evolving." A survey conducted by the Harris Poll suggests that the amount of time workers spend managing their email is closer to 14 percent. Harris Poll, "The State of Enterprise Work." Regardless, for those the Pew Research Center calls "office-based

workers" (including professionals, managers, and clerical workers), the amount of time spent on email is considerable. Purcell and Rainie, "Email and the Internet."

   3. Manjoo, "Google Wants Inbox."

6. Exercise 3

   1. Wallis, *Impacts of Media Multitasking*, 3, 4.

   2. González and Mark, " 'Constant, Constant, Multi-Tasking Crazi-ness,' " 113–120; Thompson, "Meet the Life Hackers."

   3. Rideout, Foehr, and Roberts, *Generation M2*.

   4. Jenkins, *Confronting the Challenges of Participatory Culture*, 61.

   5. Strayer and Watson, "Supertaskers and the Multitasking Brain."

   6. The Stanford report distinguishes three kinds of "media multitask-ing": "(a) between medium and face-to-face interaction; (b) between two or more media; and (c) within a single medium." Wallis, *Impacts of Media Multitasking*, 8. For a different approach, see Salvucci and Taatgen, *The Multitasking Mind*, 8–11, which locates multitasking on a continuum from concurrent to sequential activities.

   7. A variety of digital tools are now appearing that allow users to moni-tor their activities and their biological state, and serious "self-trackers" now meet at conferences on the "Quantified Self." I haven't tried to bring any of these tracking tools into my teaching. In practice, I find that the recording technologies I ask my students to install (which thus far have been available at no cost) provide enough information for people to make sophisticated observations of their own multitasking behavior.

   8. Levy, "Levy's Web site," davidmlevy.net.

   9. Ophir, Nass, and Wagner, "Cognitive Control in Media," 15583–15587.

   10. Solomon, "Eyal Ophir on the Science."

7. Exercise 4

1. Cohen, *One Who Is Not Busy*.
2. Levy et al., "Effects of Mindfulness Meditation." Interested readers can find the full results in the published paper, which is available on my Web site, Levy, "Levy's Web site," davidmlevy.net.
3. Gloria Mark's 2008 study suggests that interruptions increase the stress of work. Mark, Gudith, and Klocke, "Cost of Interrupted Work."

8. Exercise 5

1. "Sabbath Manifesto," http://www.sabbathmanifesto.org/. See also Cooper, *Fast Media, Media Fast*.
2. Hunnicutt, "Jewish Sabbath Movement"; Hunnicutt, *Work Without End*.
3. Whybrow, *American Mania*. For years, I have been exploring the acceleration of life and the role that our information technologies play in this process. Readers wanting to know more about how I understand our more-faster-better culture and the challenges it presents can consult Levy, "No Time to Think," the journal article and the video.
4. Eyal, *Hooked*.

9. Honing Our Digital Craft

1. Ingold, "Walking the Plank." Ingold actually divides craftwork into four stages: getting ready, setting out, carrying on, finishing off. I've chosen to collapse the first two into a single stage.
2. Schwartz, *Paradox of Choice*, 2.
3. McEwen, *End of Stress*, 150–151.
4. Ibid., 152.
5. Research indicates that not all forms of rest are equally effective. Stephen Kaplan, a psychologist at the University of Michigan who has

developed Attention Restoration Theory, has shown that exposure to nature is a particularly effective means of recovering our concentration when our attention muscle has fatigued. Kaplan, "Meditation, Restoration." Thus it is important to consider not just *when* to rest, but *how*.

6. Segal, Williams, and Teasdale, *Mindfulness-Based Cognitive Therapy*, 74.

7. Greenhalgh, "Progress of Captain Ludd."

10. Broadening and Deepening the Conversation

1. See the op-ed piece colleagues at Georgetown University and I wrote in the *Chronicle of Higher Education* in 2011. Levy et al., "No Cellphone? No Internet?"

2. Carr, "Does the Internet Make You Dumber?" Shirky, "Does the Internet Make You Smarter?" Carr, *Shallows;* Carr, "Is Google Making Us Stupid?"

3. reSTART, "Our Mission."

4. Carey, "A Shocker: Partisan Thought."

5. Shirky, "Why I Just Asked."

Appendix C

1. Center for Contemplative Mind, http://www.contemplativemind .org/.

2. Association for Mindfulness in Education, http://www.mindful education.org/; Mindfulness in Education Network, http://www.mindfuled .org/.

Appendix D

1. Pang, *Digital Distraction;* Rheingold, *Net Smart;* Calvo and Peters, *Positive Computing;* Gordhamer, *Wisdom 2.0*, 31.

2. Tan, *Search Inside Yourself;* Search Inside Yourself, http://siyli.org/; Wisdom 2.0 Conference, http://www.wisdom2summit.com; Eaton, "Apps for Meditation."

Appendix E

1. "Internet Gaming Disorder," http://www.dsm5.org/Documents/Internet%20Gaming%20Disorder%20Fact%20Sheet.pdf.
2. Pies, "Should DSM-V Designate"; Winkler et al., "Treatment of Internet Addiction."
3. Starcevic, "Is Internet Addiction a Useful Concept?" 16, 17.
4. Winkler et al., "Treatment of Internet Addiction," 318.

Bibliography

Association for Mindfulness in Education. "Mindfulness in Education: The Foundation for Teaching and Learning." http://www .mindfuleducation.org/.

Barley, Stephen R., Debra E. Meyerson, and Stine Grodal. "E-Mail as Source and Symbol of Stress." *Organization Science* 22, no. 4 (2011): 887–906. http://dx.doi.org/10.1287/orsc.1100.0573.

Blakeslee, Sandra, and Matthew Blakeslee. *The Body Has a Mind of Its Own: New Discoveries About How the Mind-Body Connection Helps Us Master the World.* New York: Random House, 2008.

Calvo, Rafael A., and Dorian Peters. *Positive Computing: Technology for Wellbeing and Human Potential.* Cambridge: MIT Press, 2014.

Carey, Benedict. "A Shocker: Partisan Thought Is Unconscious." *New York Times,* January 24, 2006. http://www.nytimes.com/2006/ 01/24/science/24find.html.

Carr, Nicholas. "Is Google Making Us Stupid?" *Atlantic,* July 1, 2008. http://www.theatlantic.com/magazine/archive/2008/07/is-google -making-us-stupid/6868/.

———. *The Shallows: What the Internet Is Doing to Our Brains.* New York: Norton, 2010.

———. "Does the Internet Make You Dumber?" *Wall Street Journal,*
     June 5, 2010. http://www.wsj.com/articles/SB10001424052748704
     02530457528498164479oo98.
The Center for Contemplative Mind in Society. http://www
     .contemplativemind.org/.
Cohen, Darlene. *The One Who Is Not Busy: Connecting with Work
     in a Deeply Satisfying Way.* Salt Lake City: Gibbs Smith,
     2004.
Cooper, Thomas W. *Fast Media, Media Fast: How to Clear Your Mind
     and Invigorate Your Life in an Age of Media Overload.* Boulder,
     CO: Gaeta, 2011.
Eaton, Kit. "Video Feature: Apps for Meditation and Calming on
     iPhone and Android." *New York Times,* February 25, 2015. http://
     www.nytimes.com/2015/02/26/technology/personaltech/video
     -feature-apps-for-meditation-and-calming-on-iphone-and
     -android.html.
Eyal, Nir. *Hooked: How to Build Habit-Forming Products.* New York:
     Portfolio/Penguin, 2014.
Friedman, Thomas L. *The Lexus and the Olive Tree.* New York: Farrar
     Straus Giroux, 1999.
Gill, Barry. "E-Mail: Not Dead, Evolving." *Harvard Business Review*
     91, no. 6 (2013): 32–33. https://hbr.org/2013/06/e-mail-not-dead
     -evolving/.
Goleman, Daniel. *Emotional Intelligence.* New York: Bantam, 2005.
———. *Social Intelligence: The New Science of Human Relationships.*
     New York: Bantam, 2006.
———. *Focus: The Hidden Driver of Excellence.* New York: Harper,
     2013.

González, Victor M., and Gloria Mark. "'Constant, Constant, Multi-Tasking Craziness': Managing Multiple Working Spheres." In *Proceedings of the SIGCHI Conference on Human Factors in Computing Systems,* 113–120. New York: ACM, 2004. doi:10.1145/985692.985707.

Gordhamer, Soren. *Wisdom 2.0: Ancient Secrets for the Creative and Constantly Connected.* New York: HarperOne, 2008.

Greenhalgh, Paul. "The Progress of Captain Ludd." In *The Culture of Craft: Status and Future,* ed. Peter Dormer, 104–115. New York: St. Martin's, 1997.

Harris Poll. "The State of Enterprise Work." *Workfront Resources,* 2010. http://www.workfront.com/resources/whitepaper/state-enterprise-work/.

Hunnicutt, Benjamin Kline. "The Jewish Sabbath Movement in the Early Twentieth Century." *American Jewish History* 69, no. 2 (1979): 196–225.

———. *Work Without End: Abandoning Shorter Hours for the Right to Work.* Philadelphia: Temple University Press, 1988.

Ingold, Tim. "Walking the Plank: Meditations on a Process of Skill." In *Being Alive: Essays on Movement, Knowledge, and Description,* 51–62. London: Routledge, 2011.

"Internet Gaming Disorder." http://www.dsm5.org/Documents/Internet%20Gaming%20Disorder%20Fact%20Sheet.pdf.

James, William. *The Principles of Psychology,* vol. 1. 1890; New York: Dover, 1950.

Jenkins, Henry. *Confronting the Challenges of Participatory Culture: Media Education for the 21st Century.* Cambridge: MIT Press, 2009.

Jha, Amishi P., Jason Krompinger, and Michael J. Baime. "Mindful-
    ness Training Modifies Subsystems of Attention." *Cognitive,
    Affective, and Behavioral Neuroscience* 7, no. 2 (2007): 109–119.
    doi:10.3758/CABN.7.2.109.

Jobs, Steve. "'You've Got to Find What You Love,' Jobs Says."
    Stanford University, June 14, 2005. http://news.stanford.edu/
    news/2005/june15/jobs-061505.html.

Kabat-Zinn, Jon. *Full Catastrophe Living.* New York: Dell, 1990.

Kaplan, Stephen. "Meditation, Restoration, and the Management
    of Mental Fatigue." *Environment and Behavior* 33, no. 4 (2001):
    480–506.

Laird, James D., and Sarah Strout. "Emotional Behaviors as Emo-
    tional Stimuli." In *Handbook of Emotion Elicitation and Assess-
    ment,* ed. James A. Coan and John J. B. Allen, 54–64. Oxford:
    Oxford University Press, 2007.

Levine, James A. *Get Up! Why Your Chair Is Killing You and What
    You Can Do About It.* New York: Palgrave Macmillan, 2014.

Levy, David M. *Scrolling Forward: Making Sense of Documents in the
    Digital Age.* 2001; New York: Arcade, 2016.

——. "No Time to Think: Reflections on Information Technology
    and Contemplative Scholarship." *Ethics and Information Tech-
    nology* 9, no. 4 (2007): 237–249.

——. "No Time to Think." Filmed March 5, 2008. YouTube
    video, 58:08. Posted March 7, 2008. https://www.youtube.com/
    watch?v=KHGcvj3JiGA.

——. "David Levy's Web site." davidmlevy.net.

Levy, David M., Daryl L. Nardick, Jeanine W. Turner, and Leanne
    McWatters. "No Cellphone? No Internet? So Much Less Stress."

Chronicle of Higher Education, May 8, 2011. http://chronicle
.com/article/No-Cellphone-No-Internet-So/127391/.

Levy, David M., Jacob O. Wobbrock, Alfred W. Kaszniak, and Marilyn
Ostergren. "The Effects of Mindfulness Meditation Training
on Multitasking in a High-Stress Information Environment." In
Proceedings of Graphics Interface, 45–52. Toronto: ACM, 2012.
http://dl.acm.org/citation.cfm?id=2305285.

Lutz, Antoine, Heleen A. Slagter, John D. Dunne, and Richard J.
Davidson. "Attention Regulation and Monitoring in Meditation."
Trends in Cognitive Sciences 12, no. 4 (2008): 163–169.

Manjoo, Farhad. "Google Wants Inbox to Be Your Email System for
the Next Decade." *New York Times Bits Blog.* October 22, 2014.
http://bits.blogs.nytimes.com/2014/10/22/google-unveils-inbox-a
-new-take-on-email-and-possibly-a-replacement-for-gmail/.

Mark, Gloria, Daniela Gudith, and Ulrich Klocke. "The Cost of
Interrupted Work: More Speed and Stress." In *Proceedings of the
SIGCHI Conference on Human Factors in Computing Systems,*
107–110. New York: ACM, 2008. doi:10.1145/1357054.1357072.

McEwen, Bruce. *The End of Stress as We Know It.* New York: Dana,
2002.

Mindfulness in Education Network. http://www.mindfuled.org/.

Ophir, Eyal, Clifford Nass, and Anthony D. Wagner. "Cognitive
Control in Media Multitaskers." In *Proceedings of the National
Academy of Sciences USA* 106, no. 37 (2009): 15583–15587.

Pang, Alex Soojung-Kim. *The Digital Distraction: Getting the In-
formation You Need and the Communication You Want, Without
Enraging Your Family, Annoying Your Colleagues, and Destroying
Your Soul.* New York: Little, Brown, 2013.

Parry, Marc. "You're Distracted. This Professor Can Help." *Chronicle of Higher Education,* March 24, 2013. http://chronicle.com/article/Youre-Distracted-This/138079/.

Paul, Annie Murphy. "You'll Never Learn!" *Slate* blog, May 3, 2013. http://www.slate.com/articles/health_and_science/science/2013/05/multitasking_while_studying_divided_attention_and_technological_gadgets.single.html.

Pies, Ronald. "Should DSM-V Designate 'Internet Addiction' a Mental Disorder?" *Psychiatry* 6, no. 2 (2009): 31–37.

Purcell, Kristen, and Lee Rainie. "Email and the Internet Are the Dominant Technological Tools in American Workplaces." *Pew Research Center's Internet and American Life Project.* December 30, 2014. http://www.pewinternet.org/2014/12/30/email-and-the-internet-are-the-dominant-technological-tools-in-american-workplaces/.

The Radicati Group. *Email Statistics Report, 2014–2018,* ed. Sara Radicati, April 14, 2014. http://www.radicati.com/?p=10644.

Reboot. "Sabbath Manifesto." http://www.sabbathmanifesto.org/.

reSTART. "Mission Statement." http://www.netaddictionrecovery.com/our-mission.html.

Reynolds, Gretchen. "How Exercise Could Lead to a Better Brain." *New York Times,* April 18, 2012. http://www.nytimes.com/2012/04/22/magazine/how-exercise-could-lead-to-a-better-brain.html.

Rheingold, Howard. *Net Smart: How to Thrive Online.* Cambridge: MIT Press, 2012.

Ricard, Matthieu, Antoine Lutz, and Richard J. Davidson. "Mind of the Meditator." *Scientific American* 311, no. 5 (2014): 38–45.

Richtel, Matt. "Driven to Distraction - Series." *New York Times,* n.d. http://topics.nytimes.com/top/news/technology/series/driven_to_distraction/index.html.

———. *A Deadly Wandering: A Tale of Tragedy and Redemption in the Age of Attention.* New York: William Morrow, 2014.

———. "Trying to Hit the Brake on Texting While Driving." *New York Times,* September 13, 2014. http://www.nytimes.com/2014/09/14/business/trying-to-hit-the-brake-on-texting-while-driving.html.

Rideout, V. J., U. G. Foehr, and D. F. Roberts. *Generation M2: Media in the Lives of 8–18-Year Olds.* Menlo Park, CA: Henry J. Kaiser Family Foundation, 2010.

Rosen, Larry D. *iDisorder: Understanding Our Obsession with Technology and Overcoming Its Hold on Us.* New York: Palgrave Macmillan, 2012.

Salvucci, Dario D., and Niels A. Taatgen. *The Multitasking Mind.* New York: Oxford University Press, 2011.

Sapolsky, Robert M. "Stress, Stress-Related Disease, and Emotion Regulation." In *Handbook of Emotion Regulation,* ed. James J. Gross, 606–615. New York: Guilford, 2007.

Schwartz, Barry. *The Paradox of Choice: Why More Is Less.* New York: Ecco, 2004.

Search Inside Yourself Leadership Institute. http://siyli.org/.

Segal, Zindel V., J. Mark G. Williams, and John D. Teasdale. *Mindfulness-Based Cognitive Therapy for Depression.* New York: Guilford, 2002.

Shirky, Clay. "Does the Internet Make You Smarter?" *Wall Street Journal,* June 4, 2010. http://www.wsj.com/articles/SB10001424052748704025304575284973472694334.

———. *Cognitive Surplus: How Technology Makes Consumers into Collaborators.* New York: Penguin, 2011.

———. "Why I Just Asked My Students To Put Their Laptops Away . . ." *Medium* blog. September 8, 2014. https://medium .com/@cshirky/why-i-just-asked-my-students-to-put-their -laptops-away-7f5f7c50f368.

Solomon, Avi. "Eyal Ophir on the Science of Multitasking." *Boing Boing* blog. November 7, 2011. http://boingboing.net/2011/11/07/ eyal-ophir-on-the-science-of-multitasking.html.

Starcevic, Vladan. "Is Internet Addiction a Useful Concept?" *Australian and New Zealand Journal of Psychiatry* 47, no. 1 (2013): 16–19. doi:10.1177/0004867412461693.

Stone, Linda. "Just Breathe: Building the Case for Email Apnea." *HuffPost Healthy Living* blog. February 2008. http://www .huffingtonpost.com/linda-stone/just-breathe-building-the _b_85651.html.

Strayer, David L., and Jason M. Watson. "Supertaskers and the Multitasking Brain." *Scientific American Mind* 23, no. 1 (2012): 22–29.

Tan, Chade-Meng. *Search Inside Yourself: The Unexpected Path to Achieving Success, Happiness (and World Peace).* New York: HarperOne, 2012.

Thompson, Clive. "Meet the Life Hackers." *New York Times*, October 16, 2005. http://www.nytimes.com/2005/10/16/magazine/ 16guru.html.

Wallis, Claudia. *The Impacts of Media Multitasking on Children's Learning and Development: Report from a Research Seminar.* New York: Joan Ganz Cooney Center at Sesame Workshop, 2010. http://multitasking.stanford.edu/MM_FinalReport_030510.pdf.

Whybrow, Peter C. *American Mania: When More Is Not Enough.* New York: Norton, 2005.

Wilson, Robert A., and Lucia Foglia. "Embodied Cognition." In *The Stanford Encyclopedia of Philosophy,* ed. Edward N. Zalta, 2011. http://plato.stanford.edu/archives/fall2011/entries/embodied -cognition/.

Winkler, Alexander, Deate Dorsing, Winfried Rief, Yuhui Shen, and Julia A. Gombiewski. "Treatment of Internet Addiction: A Meta-Analysis." *Clinical Psychology Review* 33, no. 2 (2013): 317–329.

Wisdom 2.0 Conference. http://www.wisdom2summit.com/.

Yates, JoAnne. *Control Through Communication: The Rise of System in American Management.* Baltimore: Johns Hopkins University Press, 1989.

Index

Note: Italic page numbers refer to material in boxes.

82; cultivation of, 39; development of, 43–44; email apnea, 38–39; and emotional state, 44, 57–59, 62–63, 64, 68, 75; Facebook use paired with, 67–68, 75, 76, 80; improvement in, 7, 9, 10, 47; impulse to check email, 20, 58–59, 76, 136; management of email, 3, 44–45, 46, 203–204n2; and meditation, 203n13; and mindful unplugging exercise, 134, 148; and multitasking, 48; overall relationship with, 62–64; and overwork, 44, 65–66; and procrastination, 58–59; quality of attention, 60–62, 64; stress of, 44, 55, 60, 62, 63, 64, 65, 66, 159; and task focus, 19, 20, 23; time spent on, 168; and triggers, 36, 57, 58, 68, 71, 72, 75, 76–77, 114. *See also* Email observation exercise; Focused email exercise

Embodied cognition, 203n9

Emotional balance: and email use, 45, 46, 159; and exercise, 38; and online activities, 3, 5, 27, 34–36; and self-observation, 4; and task focus, 20, 22

Emotional state: and email use, 44, 57–59, 62–63, 64, 68, 75; mindful check-in, 41, 50, 187, 188, 189; and multitasking, 100, 103, 104, 105–106, 107

Emotions: and discussions, 175, 176–177; low-level emotions, 4; and productivity, 20; and stress response, 34–36. *See also* Triggers

Engagement, 15, 22, 169, 179

Engelbart, Douglas, 5–6

Escapism, 144

Exercise and movement, 37, 38

Exercises: as experiments, 15–16; overview of, 23–25; six-part structure of, 24, 25; use of, 13–14. *See also* Email observation exercise; Focused email exercise; Focused multitasking exercise; Multitasking observation exercise

Facebook: addiction to, 196; and attention, 3; email use compared to, 45; email use paired with, 67–68, 75, 76, 80; improvement in use of, 9; and mindful unplugging exercise, 134, 138–139, 141, 144, 145, 147, 148; profits from advertising, 151; as substitute for email, 45–46, 69; and task focus, 20, 41

Face-to-face interactions, 34, 65, 88, 95, 117, 141, 204n6

Facial expressions, 38

Fast World, xi–xii, 164–166

Fight-or-flight response. *See* Stress response

Flaming, 34